Handmade Underground
KNITWEAR

25 Fun Projects for All Occasions

Laura Long and Melissa Halvorson
with additional projects by
Staceyjoy Elkin and Kim Hamlin

WILEY
wiley.com

CONTENTS

INTRODUCTION

Welcome to the world of indie style crafters—the place where haute couture meets street culture, where beloved crafts of yesteryear are taken up by young, edgy trendsetters, and where anything goes.

Packed with 25 stylish knitting projects, *Handmade Underground Knitwear* is all about striving for something that can't be bought—individuality. Nothing else can match the satisfaction you gain from making something by hand. When you knit, you're not just constructing a garment, you're investing hours of your life into something unique. We hope these exciting projects dreamt up and designed by Laura, Melissa, Stacey, and Kim will inspire you to get creative and adventurous with your knitting.

In the following pages you will find a range of fabulous knitwear suitable for knitters of all levels. Dress up with shrugs, legwarmers, and long fingerless mitts; dress down with loungewear to long for, from smocks to slippers; and dress warm with snug hats, scarves, and mittens to make you wish it was winter all year round. Each project comes with clear step-by-step instructions to guide you and beautiful photography to inspire you, plus charts and illustrations where needed. Chapter 1 contains detailed instructions for the stitches and techniques used throughout the book.

So, if you hate the idea of looking just like everyone else and love re-inventing yourself and your outfit, you're ready for *Handmade Underground Knitwear*.

Grab your knitting needles and let's get started!

TIPS & TECHNIQUES
CHAPTER 1

This chapter covers all the stitches and techniques needed to create the projects in this book, starting with the basics of choosing the yarn and tension (tightness of the stitching) appropriate for each project. Step-by-step instructions illustrated with clear diagrams show how to cast on (make stitches to get started) and bind off (permanently finish your work) and guide you through the basic stitch patterns that you will need. More complex stitches and techniques are also clearly explained and illustrated. Some garments are knitted in sections and then joined together in various ways, and the most common of these techniques are set out here. Plus there's information on how to block and steam your finished items to prepare them for wearing.

The knitting patterns in this book use abbreviations for stitches, techniques, and instructions so a complete list of those used is given on page 25 for you to refer back to as you work through the book.

If you're a beginning knitter, why not start by practicing the basic stitches and techniques from this chapter with scrap yarn until you are confident in keeping the tension even, before moving on to the projects themselves. You'll find a range of items, suitable for all skill levels, so you can build up your expertise. In no time at all, you will be creating unique, handmade pieces of fabulous knitwear. For those with more experience and keen for a bit more of a challenge, there are plenty of projects here to tempt you, plus speedier pieces for days when you need to to whip up something special in a flash.

Each project is graded according to its level of difficulty: one star for simple and straightforward patterns; two stars for intermediate projects; and three stars for more complex patterns.

Yarns

There are many different types of yarn available in all varieties of texture and color.

Yarns are suggested for each project, but feel free to change these if you don't like them or can't find them locally or online. However, if you do decide to use a different yarn, be sure to choose one that is of the same thickness and works to the same number of stitches and rows to the inch, as noted in the selected project's Gauge entry. You want the tension to be as close to the pattern as possible. Otherwise you might end up with a finished project that is too big or too small.

Gauge/Tension

On each ball of yarn you will find tension information that indicates how many stitches and rows are recommended for the yarn, a specified number of inches, usually (but not always) over 4 in. (10cm). The tension will change depending on the size (thickness) of needles you use and the weight, or thickness, of the yarn that you knit with. The gauge for each yarn selected in this book is given at the start of a project. When knitting garments, it is important to match the recommended gauge to avoid knitting a garment that is too big or too small. When knitting scarves this tension is less important.

Before beginning a project, always make a sample swatch with the number of stitches and

Lace pattern with a twisted rib

rows specified in the Gauge entry with the needles recommended and measure it carefully. If your swatch measures more than the number of inches specified, make another swatch with smaller needles. If your swatch is smaller than specified, make a new swatch with larger needles. Keep trying different size needles until you get as close as possible to the specified gauge.

Selecting needle size

All knitting patterns give suggested needle sizes. The needle size will vary depending on the thickness of yarn or desired tension. Some patterns use knitting needles that are bigger or smaller than you would expect. Fine yarn knitted on larger needles gives a more open look. Thick yarn knitted on thinner needles will result in a more solid piece of knitting.

Holding the Yarn

There are several ways to hold yarn and everyone picks up a different technique that works best for them. One method follows. If you're left-handed, hold the yarn the same way, but in your left hand.

Hold the yarn in your right hand over your little finger and under your third finger, under your center finger and over your index finger (Fig. 1). The tension of the yarn is controlled by your little finger. Holding the yarn this way may not be the most comfortable for you though, so experiment until you find what works for you.

Fig. 1

Holding the Needles

The right needle is either held like a pencil or with your hand over the top of it. Again, experiment until you find what is comfortable for you. The left needle is held slightly over the right one. The tip of the needle is controlled by the thumb and index finger.

Casting On

1. Make a slip knot as follows: Pull 12 in (30.5cm) length of yarn from the skein. Lay the end on a table and loop the attached yarn over it. Place the attached yarn under the the loop. Place your needle under the bottom strand (Fig. 2) and pull on both ends of the yarn to complete the slip knot. Hold the needle with the slip knot in your left hand.

Fig. 2

2. Insert the right needle through the slip knot from left to right and wrap the yarn around the tip of the right needle from left to right (Fig. 3).

Fig. 3

3. Pull the loop through the slip knot but DO NOT slip the new stitch off the left needle (Fig. 4).

Fig. 4

4. Insert the left needle from right to left through new stitch on right needle (Fig. 4) and slip the new stitch off the right needle and onto the left needle.

5. Insert the right needle between the slip knot and the first stitch and wrap the yarn around the right needle (Fig. 5).

Fig. 5

6. Draw the loop through and place it on the left needle in same manner as the first stitch.

Repeat steps 5 and 6, always working between the last two stitches on the left needle, until you reach the required number of cast on stitches. This method of casting on is known as the cable cast on or short tail cast on. It ceates a firm, but elastic edge.

Knit Stitch

1. Hold the needle with the cast on stitches in your left hand and make sure that the yarn is at the back of the work. Insert the right needle through the front of the first stitch from left to right (Fig. 6).

Fig. 6

2. Wrap the yarn from left to right over the tip of the right needle (Fig. 7).

Fig. 7

3. Pull the new loop on the right needle through the stitch on the left needle (Fig. 8).

Fig. 8

4. Slip the stitch off the left needle keeping the new stitch on the right needle. One knit stitch is complete (Fig. 9).

Fig. 9

5. Repeat steps 1–4 until all the stitches have been transferred from the left needle to the right needle. At the end of the row, swap the needle with the stitches to your left

hand and work the next row in the same manner. Before beginning a new row, be sure that the yarn hangs straight down from the top of the work. Try this for a few rows.

Garter Stitch

Knitting every row, as you have been doing, is called Garter stitch. It looks the same on both sides and it doesn't roll at the edges. It is great for making scarves.

Garter stitch

Purl Stitch

1. Hold the needle with the stitches (cast-on stitches shown in this example) in your left hand and insert the right needle through the front of the first stitch from right to left (Fig. 10).

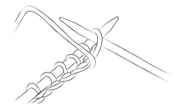

Fig. 10

2. Wrap the yarn from right to left behind the tip of the right needle (Fig. 11).

Fig. 11

3. Pull the new loop on the right hand needle through the stitch on the left hand needle (Fig. 12).

Fig. 12

4. Slip the stitch off the left needle keeping the new stitch on the right needle. One purl stitch is complete.

5. Repeat steps 1–4 until all the stitches have been transferred from the left needle to the right needle. At the end of the row, swap the needle with the stitches into your left hand and work the next row. Try this for a few rows. Purling every row also produces Garter stitch.

Stockinette Stitch

Stockinette stitch is the most common stitch used in knitted pieces.

The first row is made using the knit stitch and the second row using the purl stitch. These two rows are repeated to create a flat piece of knitting. Stockinette stitch fabric is smooth on one side and bumpy on the opposite side. The fabric curls in at the side edges until it is seamed.

Binding Off

These are the most common bind off methods.

Knitwise

1. Knit two stitches. Place the tip of the left needle through the front of the first stitch on the right needle (Fig. 13).

2. Lift the first stitch over the second stitch and drop it off the needle (Fig. 14). The remaining stitch stays on the right needle.

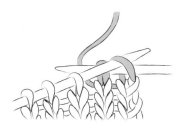

Fig. 13

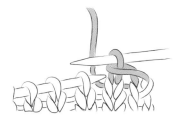

Fig. 14

3. Knit the next stitch. Lift the first stitch over the second stitch and off the needle. Repeat steps 2 and 3 until one stitch remains.

4. Cut the yarn and pull it through the final stitch to close it (fasten off).

Purlwise

1. Purl two stitches. Place the tip of the left needle through the front of the first stitch on the right needle.

2. Lift the first stitch over the second stitch and off the right needle.

3. Purl the next stitch. Lift the first stitch over the second stitch and drop it off the needle. Repeat steps 2 and 3 until one stitch remains.

4. Cut the yarn and pull it through the final stitch to close it (fasten off).

Decreasing Stitches

Decrease stitches to help shape your knitting and change the number of stitches on your needle(s). This can be achieved in several ways.

K2tog – knit two stitches together.

Knit the next two stitches together as though they were a single stitch (Fig. 15). This results in a right-slanting decrease.

Fig. 15

Skp – slip 1, knit 1, pass slipped stitch over.

Slip the next stitch knitwise onto the right needle (Fig. 16), knit the next stitch, lift the slipped stitch over the knitted stitch and off the needle. This results in a left-slanting decrease.

Fig. 16

Ssk – Slip 2 stitches separately knitwise to right needle (Fig. 16).

Insert left needle into the front of the two slipped sts and knit them together by wrapping the yarn around the tip of the right hand needle that's in back of the work (Fig. 17). This results in a left-slanting decrease (Fig. 18).

Fig. 17

Fig. 18

Dbl Dec – Centered Double Decrease.

Slip 2 stitches together knitwise, k1, lift the slipped sts over the knitted stitch (Fig. 19)

Fig. 19

and off the right needle. This results in a left-slanting decrease.

Increasing Stitches

Increase stitches to gain a stitch and help shape your

knitting. This can be achieved in several ways.

Kfb – Knit into Front and Back

Knit into the next stitch on the left needle (Fig. 20) but instead of removing it, knit into

Fig. 20

Centered Double Decrease

Fig. 21

Fig. 23

Fig. 26

it again through the back loop (Fig. 21). Slip the original stitch off the left needle.

Pfb – Purl into Front and Back

Purl into the front and into the back of the next stitch.

M1 or M1L – Make 1 or Make 1 Left

Insert the left needle under the horizontal strand between the stitches from front to back (Fig. 22), then knit into the back of the strand (Figs. 23 and 24).

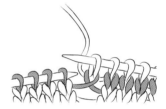

Fig. 24

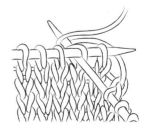

Fig. 27

M1R – Make 1 Right

Insert the left needle under the horizontal strand between the stitches from back to front (Fig. 25), then knit into the front of the strand (Figs. 26 and 27).

Twists

RT – Right Twist

Knit into the front of the second stitch on the left needle (Fig. 28), knit the first stitch, then drop both stitches from the left needle at the same time.

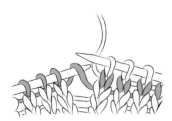

Fig. 22

Fig. 25

Fig. 28

Alternate Right Twist – Knit two stitches together, but do not drop from left needle, knit first stitch again (Fig. 29), then drop both stitches from needle.

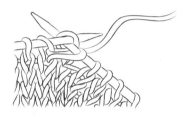

Fig. 29

LT – Left Twist

Knit into the back of the second stitch on the needle (Fig. 30) and then knit into the front of the first stitch. Then drop both stitches from the left needle.

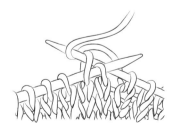

Fig. 30

Alternate Left Twist – Knit two stitches together through the back loops, but do not drop from left needle. Knit the first stitch again from the front, dropping both stitches from needle.

Cables

Cables involve transposing the position of multiple stitches in your fabric, creating a twist of more than two stitches. To work a left twisting cable, slip the specified number of stitches onto a cable needle (a very short, usually bent, needle with points at both ends) and hold it in the front or back of your work (Fig. 31), as noted in the instructions. Knit the specified number of stitches from the left needle, then knit the stitches from the cable needle making sure that the first stitch you knit is the first one that you slipped onto the cable needle (Fig. 32).

Cable stitch

To work a right twisting cable, repeat as before, holding the specified number of stitches on the cable needle in back of your work.

Cable abbreviations are broken down as follows:

C = cable

= the total number of stitches involved in the cable. Half of this number will be slipped to the cable needle.

B or F = where to hold the cable needle, either in Back or in Front of work.

Therefore, C4F would mean to slip two stitches to the cable needle and hold it in front of work (Fig. 31), knit two from left needle, then knit the two stitches from the cable needle (Fig. 32).

Likewise, C4B means to slip two stitches to the cable needle and hold it in back of work (Fig. 33), knit two from left needle, then knit the two stitches from the cable needle (Fig. 34).

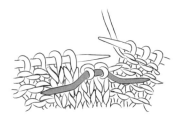

Fig. 31

Fig. 32

Fig. 33

Fig.34

Yarn Overs

Yarn overs are another form of increasing a stitch. A yarn over creates a small hole in the fabric. Yarn overs are used extensively in lace knitting and are usually paired with decreases.

When a yarn over falls before a knit stitch, bring the yarn forward between the needles, then back over the top of the right needle to be in position to knit the next stitch (Fig. 35).

Fig. 35

Wrapping Stitches

Slip next stitch purlwise. With yarn in front, slip same stitch back to left needle. Turn and work next row. When instructed to knit the wrapped stitch, lift the wrap onto the left needle and knit the wrap with the stitch wrapped.

Picking Up Stitches

Insert the needle from the front to the back under two strands at the edge of the worked piece (Fig. 36). Wrap the yarn around the needle as if to knit, then bring the needle with the yarn back through the piece to the right side, resulting in a stitch on the needle. Repeat evenly spaced along the edge, picking up the specified number of stitches.

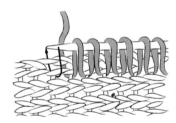

Fig. 36

Knitting on Circular or Double Pointed Needles

Circular and double pointed needles are for knitting tubular work. You knit around the needles without creating any seams. It is important to remember (or mark) the starting point, especially if you are knitting a pattern.

With a circular needle, cast on and spread the stitches evenly along the entire length of the needle. Make sure that the length of cast-on stitches isn't twisted because it is impossible to untwist the knitting once you start. Begin by knitting the first cast on stitch (Fig. 37).

Continue knitting around to form a tube.

With double pointed needles, cast on and divide the stitches evenly among the needles. If you are knitting with four

Fig. 37

needles, divide the stitches among three needles, leaving the fourth needle free; if you are knitting with five needles, divide the stitches among four needles, leaving the fifth needle free. Making sure the work is not twisted, use the free needle to knit across the first needle (Fig. 38).

Use the free needle to knit across the next needle. Continue around in the same manner.

To achieve Stockinette stitch on circular or double pointed needles, knit every round. To achieve Garter stitch, alternate knit and purl rounds.

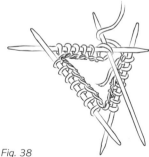

Fig. 38

Color Pattern Knitting

Knitting that involves two or more colors—with each color feeding from a different ball—is often called Fair Isle knitting when there's there's a distinct repeating pattern. You change colors by dropping one yarn strand and making the next stitch with a yarn that's a different color. Strands of the unused color(s) are not cut between the stitches. Floats (the loops of yarn at the back of the knitting) will be created (Fig. 39).

Fig.39

Knit along the row in your first color until you come to the stitch where you want to change the color. Insert the right needle through the next stitch and pull the new yarn

through to create the stitch. It is important not to pull the stitches too tight or the stranded knitting will pull in and become too tight and pucker.

Using a pattern grid for Fair Isle

Fair Isle patterns are usually shown on a charted grid, so it is easy to see what the pattern looks like. Start at the bottom of the chart and work up. Each line represents a new row. Every square represents a stitch and color. On right side rows, always follow the chart from right to left; on wrong side rows, follow the chart from left to right. If working in rounds, always follow the chart from right to left.

Seaming Knitting

Always use the same yarn that you used to knit with so that the stitches don't show. If you knit the project with two strands of yarn, only use one strand for seaming.

Blunt-tipped tapestry needles are best because they don't cut split the stitches.

Running stitch

With the right sides of both pieces facing and a needle threaded with a single strand of yarn, make small straight stitches along the knitting edge, one stitch at a time, passing the needle over one knitted stitch and under the next (through both knitted layers)to create a dashed line. Be careful that you sew as straight and as close to the edge as possible.

Mattress stitch (vertical weaving)

With the right sides of both pieces facing and the edges even, sew through both pieces once to secure the seam. Insert the needle under the bar between the first and second stitches on the row of one piece and pull the yarn through (Fig. 40). Insert the needle under the next two bars on the second piece. Insert the needle under the next two bars on the first piece. Repeat from side to side, being careful to match rows. If the edges are different lengths, it may be necessary to insert the needle under one bar on the shorter edge.

Fig. 40

Horizontal weaving

With the right sides of both pieces facing up and the edges even, bring the yarn needle from behind the work and through the center of the first stitch. Bring the needle over the top of the matched edges and insert it under both loops of the corresponding stitch on the second piece (Fig. 41). Bring

the needle back over the seam and insert in the center of the same stitch, then bring it up through the center of the next stitch. Repeat in the same manner across, maintaining tension.

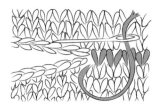

Fig. 41

Whipstitch

With right sides together and the edges even, sew through both pieces to secure the beginning of the seam. Insert the needle from right to left through both pieces (Fig. 42). Bring the needle around and insert it from right to left through both pieces again. Repeat the stitch in the same manner, evenly spaced, along the edge.

Fig. 42

Grafting (Kitchener Stitch)

Grafting, or Kitchener stitch, is a way to finish a piece so that the seam looks like a continuous row, leaving no ridge on the inside of the work.

To set up for grafting, gently pull the waste yarn from your piece(s) or pull the needle out of your last row of work, thus exposing live stitches. Lay the pieces right sides up on a table with the live stitch edges together.

1. Insert the tapestry needle through the first live stitch on the bottom piece knitwise (Fig. 43).

Fig. 43

2. Insert the tapestry needle through the second stitch on the bottom piece purlwise (Fig. 44).

Fig. 44

3. Insert the tapestry needle through the first stitch on the top piece purlwise (Fig. 45).

Fig. 45

4. Insert the tapestry needle through the second stitch on top piece knitwise (Fig. 46).

Fig. 46

Repeat steps 1–4 until all of the stitches have been worked, taking care that the sewn stitches aren't tighter or looser than the knitted stitches.

Stitch Holders

You can use a variety of knitting tools for holding stitches that are to be saved in order to be knitted later. You can thread spare yarn through the stitches or slip the stitches onto double pointed needles or circular needles. Safety pin type stitch holders work well because they prevent the stitches from falling off.

Blanket Stitch

Thread a tapestry needle with a contrasting color yarn. Holding the yarn tail (the end of the yarn) at the edge of the piece, insert the needle through the knitted fabric at point A, and bring it up at point B (edge of the piece) catching the loop of the yarn underneath the needle (Fig. 47).

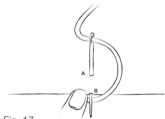

Fig. 47

Insert the needle though the fabric at the next point A and bring it up at the next point B, catching the loop of yarn (Fig. 48). Repeat along the edge; fasten off.

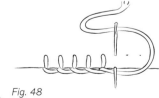

Fig. 48

Crocheting

It is helpful for knitters to know the following basic crochet stitches because they are great for finishing edges.

Single Crochet

Insert the crochet hook in the stitch indicated, yarn over and pull the loop through the stitch, yarn over and draw it through both loops on the hook (Fig. 49).

Fig. 49

Crab Stitch

Make a single crochet by inserting the crochet hook into the stitch indicated in your project instructions and then completing the stitch as explained above. All the subsequent stitches are single crochet, but worked in the opposite direction, as follows: Working from left to right, *insert the hook into the stitch to the right of hook (Fig. 50). Yarn over and draw the loop through the stitch, yarn over again and draw this loop through both loops that are already on the hook; repeat from * along the edge until you reach the location noted in the instructions.

Fig. 50

Blocking

Your knitwear will need to be shaped, or blocked, before it is ready to wear. Follow the instructions on yarn labels or block as follows:

Wool – steam the item on a light setting, supporting the weight of the iron at all times. Work the piece to the desired shape, pinning it in place as needed. Allow to dry flat, away from heat or sunlight.

Synthetic and blends – submerge the item in cool water. Roll the piece in a clean terry towel and gently press out the excess moisture. Lay the piece flat and allow it to dry completely, away from heat and sunlight.

Some projects in the book require slightly different blocking treatment, and this is given where applicable.

Knitting and Crochet Abbreviations

[ ] or ( ) work instructions within brackets or parentheses as many times as directed or work instructions in the stitch indicated

Abbreviation	Description
C	cable
CB	cable back
CC	contrast color
CF	cable front
dec(s)	decrease(s)/decreasing
DK	double knitting
dpn(s)	double pointed needle(s)
inc(s)	increase(s)/increasing
k or K	knit
k2tog	knit two stitches together
kfb	knit into front and back of stitch
kwise	knitwise
LT	left twist
m1	make one stitch
m1l	make one left
m1r	make one right
MC	main color
p or P	purl
p2tog	purl two stitches together
psso	pass slipped stitch over
pwise	purlwise
rnd(s)	round(s)
RS	right side
RT	right twist
skp	slip one, knit one, pass stitch over—one stitch decreased
sl	slip
ssk	slip, slip, knit these two stitches together—one stitch decreased
st(s)	stitch(es)
St st	Stockinette stitch
tbl	through back loop
tog	together
WS	wrong side
wyib	with yarn in back
wyif	with yarn in front
yo	yarn over

Asterisks in patterns

Asterisks (*) occur when parts of the pattern need to be repeated in the same row. Repeat from the asterisk as many times as the instructions indicate.

DRESSING UP
CHAPTER 2

It's amazing how the right accessory can enliven a plain everyday outfit, and for true Handmade Underground style nothing beats making your own. These projects are the perfect way to instantly transform your ensemble, whether you're smartening up your everyday wear or heading out for the evening. Most of these projects are straightforward to make and suitable for beginning and intermediate knitters. If you're keen to take on more of a challenge, try your hand at the gorgeous Belladonna Mitts.

The projects:

The Isabela Bolero is perfect for summer evenings, and allows you to add a bit of color to your outfit without the challenge of changing yarns, while for punked-up glamour, nothing beats the Belladonna Opera-Length Fingerless Mitts. Legwarmers are making a comeback, and don't think aerobics classes or 80s musicals; these Hook-and-Eye Clover Legwarmers are the perfect modern accessory for a dress and heels. With its beautiful button details, the Nine of Diamonds Capelet is gorgeous to look at and super-practical for cold days too. If you're looking for a quick and easy way to add a unique edge to your style, the Ribbed Flowers are simple to make so you can have a great range of shapes and colors to liven up your wardrobe in no time. The Midnight Cable Scarf is brilliantly thick—not only will it keep you warm day and night, but it can be dressed up and down to suit your mood. A modern take on an old classic, the Lauren Woven Belt works just as well with baggy, loose-fitting jeans as it does with a dress, while the Jutta Beret is a striking hat that will go with any outfit. For a soft and luxurious way to keep warm, the Chrysalis Shrug is the ideal project to try. Whatever the occasion, these knitted accessories are the way to show off your style and create an eye-catching look that's all your own.

ISABELA BOLERO

This bolero is ideal for keeping you warm on cool summer evenings. The beautiful multi-colored yarn adds an interesting effect without the challenge of changing colors, and the dainty lace pattern provides texture and style. The finishing required for this project is minimal because the sleeves and collar are knit in the round.

Skill level ★ ★

Yarn

- Sirdar Escape Ecstasy #0187 [51% wool, 49% acrylic; 120 yds. (110m)/50g]—3 balls

Needles and Notions

- US size 8 16 in. and 29 in. circular needles
- 2 yds. smooth scrap yarn
- Stitch marker
- Tapestry needle

Gauge

- 18 sts and 27 rows = 4 in. (10cm) in St st

Size

- 23½ in. (60cm) wide x 12½ in. (32cm) long, unstretched
- One size fits most

Pattern notes

The bolero is knit in 2 pieces from the bottom of the sleeve to the center of the back. The center back is seamed, then a ribbed edging is added around the neck.

First Side

Using shorter circular needles, cast on 70 sts. Join, being careful not to twist.

Rnd 1: knit around.

Rnd 2: *k1, k2tog, yo, k1, yo, skp, k1; repeat from * across.

Rnd 3: knit around.

Rnd 4: *k2tog, yo, k3, yo, skp; repeat from * around.

Rnds 5–32: repeat rnds 1–4, 7 times.

Rnd 33: knit around.

Begin working in rows.

Row 1 (Back): *k1, k2tog, yo, k1, yo, skp, k1; repeat from * 3 times more. Slip 28 sts just worked onto scrap length of yarn. Continue across remaining sts in pattern—42 sts.

Row 2: purl across.

Row 3: *k2tog, yo, k3, yo, skp; repeat from * across.

Row 4: purl across.

Row 5: *k1, k2tog, yo, k1, yo, skp, k1; repeat from * across.

Rows 6–40: Repeat rows 2–5, 8 times, then repeat rows 2–4 once more.

Bind off all sts.

Second Side

Work same as First Side through rnd 33.

Begin working in rows.

Row 1 (Back): *k1, k2tog, yo, k1, yo, skp, k1; repeat from * 6 times more. Slip next 28 sts onto scrap length of yarn—42 sts.

Complete same as First Side.

Weave bound off edges together.

Edging

With longer circular needles and beginning at center back seam pick up 40 sts across to st holder, slip sts from scrap yarn to needle and knit across, pick up 80 sts evenly spaced across to next scrap yarn, slip sts from scrap yarn to needle and knit across, pick up 40 sts evenly spaced across to center back, place marker to mark beginning of rnd—216 sts.

Rnds 1–10: *k2, p2; repeat from * around.

Bind off all sts in ribbing.

Finishing

Weave in loose ends.

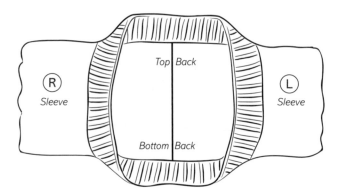

BELLADONNA OPERA-LENGTH FINGERLESS MITTS

These mitts are an exercise in warmth and a bit of tricky knitting. Wear them over thin black lambskin gloves, or to accompany a glamorous evening dress. They'll keep you warm when riding your bike to the ball. The Fair Isle pattern running up the top of the arm is fabulous for using up small balls of leftover yarn.

Skill level ★ ★ ★

Yarn

- KnitPicks Palette Black #23729 (MC) [100% Peruvian Highland Wool; 231 yds. (210m)/50g]—1 ball (used double strand)
- KnitPicks Andean Treasure Mystery Heather #23494 (Color A) [100% baby alpaca; 110 yds. (100m)/50g]—1 ball
- 6 assorted contrasting colors (Colors B–G) that work to the same gauge as main colors—12 yds. (11m) each
- 1 yd. (1m) smooth, heavy weight waste yarn

Needles and Notions

- US size 7 (4.5mm) straight needles
- Crochet hook: US-F/5 (3.5mm)
- Tapestry needle

Gauge

- Holding 2 strands of MC, 16 sts and 20 rows = 4 in. (10cm) in St st

Size

- 8¾ in. (22cm) circumference at widest point x 17¼ in. (44cm) long

Pattern notes

These close-fitting mitts are a bit challenging as they're knit sideways. Asymmetrical shaping is done only on the palm side of the mitts by using short rows.

The pattern begins and ends with waste yarn.

Left Mitt

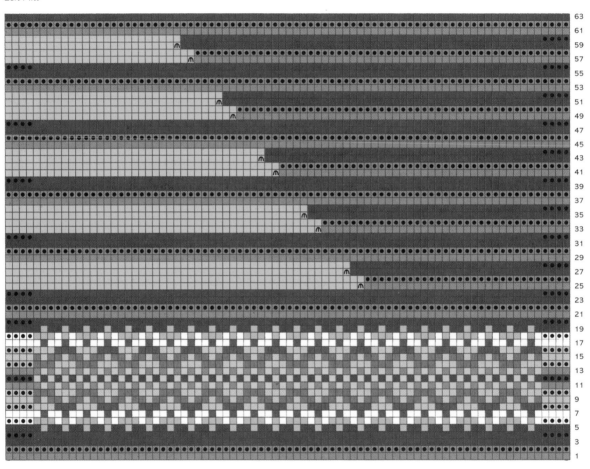

On RS rows work Chart
from right to left; On WS
rows work Chart from
left to right.
Knit on RS rows, purl on
WS rows (except as
marked otherwise), in
color indicated.

 MC (2 strands)

▨	color A
▨	color B
▨	color C
▨	color D
▨	color E
☐	color F

☐	color G
☐	unworked stitches
●	knit on WS row
⋔	wrap stitch and turn, leaving remaining stitches unworked

Left Mitt

With waste yarn, cast on 80 sts, and knit one row. Cut waste yarn.

Rows 1 and 2: with Color A, knit across.

Row 3 (RS): with MC, knit across.

Row 4: with MC, k4 (border), purl across to last 4 sts (border) k4.

Rows 5–19: work center 72 sts in St st, following chart, maintaining 4 sts in garter st (knit every row) at each edge.

Row 20: with MC, k4, purl across to last 4 sts, k4.

Rows 21 and 22: with Color A, knit across.

Row 23: with MC, knit across.

Row 24: k4, purl across to last 4 sts, k4.

Row 25: with Color A, k29, wrap next st; turn, leaving remaining sts unworked.

Note: Leave remaining sts unworked after wrap st on every short row.

Row 26: knit across.

Row 27: with MC, k31, wrap next st; turn.

Row 28: purl across to last 4 sts, k4.

Rows 29 and 30: with Color A, knit across all sts.

Row 31: with MC, knit across.

Row 32: k4, purl across to last 4 sts, k4.

Row 33: with Color A, k35, wrap next st; turn.

Row 34: knit across.

Row 35: with MC, k37, wrap next st; turn.

Row 36: purl across to last 4 sts, k4.

Rows 37 and 38: with Color A, knit across all sts.

Row 39: with MC, knit across.

Row 40: k4, purl across to last 4 sts, k4.

Row 41: with Color A, k41, wrap next st; turn.

Row 42: knit across.

Row 43: with MC, k43, wrap next st; turn.

Row 44: purl across to last 4 sts, k4.

Rows 45 and 46: with Color A, knit across all sts.

Row 47: with MC, knit across.

Row 48: k4, purl across to last 4 sts, k4.

Row 49: with Color A, k47, wrap next st; turn.

Row 50: knit across.

Row 51: with MC, k49, wrap next st; turn.

Row 52: purl across to last 4 sts, k4.

Rows 53 and 54: with Color A, knit across all sts.

Row 55: with MC, knit across.

Row 56: k4, p across to last 4 sts, k4.

Row 57: with Color A, k53, wrap next st; turn.

Row 58: knit across.

Row 59: with MC, k55, wrap next st; turn.

Row 60: purl across to last 4 sts, k4.

Rows 61 and 62: with Color A, knit across all sts.

Row 63: with MC, knit across.

Knit one row in waste yarn.

Right Mitt

With waste yarn, cast on 80 sts, and knit one row. Cut waste yarn.

For Right Mitt Chart, see page 36.

Rows 1 and 2: with Color A, knit across.

Row 3: with MC, knit across.

Row 4: k4, purl across to last 4 sts, k4.

Row 5: with Color A, k55, wrap next st; turn.

Row 6: knit across.

Right Mitt

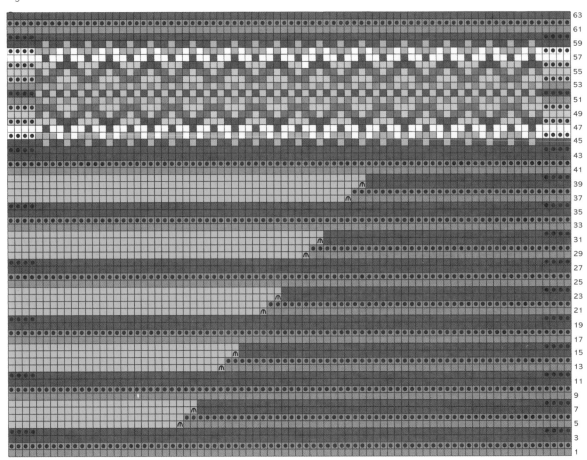

On RS rows work Chart
from right to left; On WS
rows work Chart from
left to right.
Knit on RS rows, purl on
WS rows (except as
marked otherwise), in
color indicated.

■ MC (2 strands)

■	color A
■	color B
■	color C
■	color D
■	color E
□	color F

□	color G
□	unworked stitches
●	knit on WS row
⋔	wrap stitch and turn, leaving remaining stitches unworked

Row 7: with MC, k53, wrap next st; turn.

Row 8: purl across to last 4 sts, k4.

Rows 9 and 10: with Color A, knit across all sts.

Row 11: with MC, knit across.

Row 12: k4, purl across to last 4 sts, k4.

Row 13: with Color A, k49, wrap next st; turn.

Row 14: knit across.

Row 15: with MC, k47, wrap next st; turn.

Row 16: purl across to last 4 sts, k4.

Rows 17 and 18: with Color A, knit across all sts.

Row 19: with MC, knit across.

Row 20: k4, purl across to last 4 sts, k4.

Row 21: with Color A, k43, wrap next st; turn.

Row 22: knit across.

Row 23: with MC, k41, wrap next st; turn.

Row 24: purl across to last 4 sts, k4.

Rows 25 and 26: with Color A, knit across all sts.

Row 27: with MC, knit across.

Row 28: k4, purl across to last 4 sts, k4.

Row 29: with Color A, k37,

wrap next st; turn.

Row 30: knit across.

Row 31: with MC, k35, wrap next st; turn.

Row 32: purl across to last 4 sts, k4.

Rows 33 and 34: with Color A, knit across all sts.

Row 35: with MC, knit across.

Row 36: k4, purl across to last 4 sts, k4.

Row 37: with Color A, k31, wrap next st; turn.

Row 38: knit across.

Row 39: with MC, k29, wrap next st; turn.

Row 40: purl across to last 4 sts, k4.

Rows 41 and 42: with Color A, knit across all sts.

Row 43: with MC, knit across.

Row 44: k4, purl across to last 4 sts, k4.

Rows 45–59: work center 72 sts in St st, following chart, and maintaining 4 sts in garter st at each edge.

Row 60: with MC, k4, purl across to last 4 sts, k4.

Rows 61 and 62: with Color A, knit across.

Row 63: with MC, knit across.

Knit one row in waste yarn.

Finishing

Weave in loose ends, taking care not to weave ends in waste yarn edges. Lightly steam the wrong side of the work, making sure to include the waste yarn edges. This will make it much easier to graft.

With MC and beginning at narrow edge, graft 12 stitches together, removing waste yarn as you proceed. Cut yarn.

Beginning at opposite edge, graft edges together, leaving last 11 stitches open for thumb, and removing waste yarn as you proceed; do NOT cut yarn or fasten off.

Insert crochet hook into next free stitch on thumb opening and work single crochet in this stitch and in each of the next 10 stitches, single crochet in the side of the grafted stitches, single crochet in the next 11 open stitches on second side, single crochet in the edge of the grafted stitches, slip stitch in the first single crochet to join; cut yarn and pull though loop on hook.

Weave in loose ends. Wash in lukewarm water and block flat.

HOOK-AND-EYE CLOVER LEGWARMERS

Designed to form a union between ultimate functionality and Neo-Victorian flirtatiousness, the open lace stitch and delicate hook-and-eye closure transform ordinary legwarmers into a subtle suggestion of what may lie beneath. Wear them low and slouchy with the back opening adjusted to allow for any heel height.

Skill level ★ ★

Yarn

- Malabrigo Worsted Pearl Ten #69 [100% merino wool; 215 yds. (195m)/100g]—1 hank

Needles and Notions

- US size 9 (5.5mm) straight needles
- 1 yard 100% cotton hook-and-eye tape (dyed to desired color)
- Sewing needle and thread (to match yarn)
- Tapestry needle
- Pins

Gauge

- 16 sts and 20 rows = 4 in. (10cm) in St st

Size

- 10½ in. (26.5cm) circumference x 15 in. (38cm) long

Pattern notes

These legwarmers are worked in rows from bottom to top. The lace stitch looks complex but it's just a few simple decreases and increases worked on RS rows.

Blocking is very important for this project, as with all lace patterns; it will give you extra length and your pieces will drape properly. Be careful not to stretch the ribbing, however, as that could make the legwarmers too wide.

On RS rows, work Chart from right to left; On WS rows, work Chart from left to right.

☐	Repeat instructions enclosed in box as many times as specified in written instructions
☐	knit on RS rows; purl on WS rows
/	k2tog—knit next 2 sts together
\	skp—slip 1 kwise, k1, pass slipped st over
○	yo—yarn over
●	purl on RS rows; knit on WS rows

Cast on 42 sts.

Proceed by following Chart or written instructions.

Row 1: purl across.

Row 2: k2, p38, k2.

Row 3: k4, yo, k2, skp, k2tog, k2, yo, *k1, yo, k2, skp, k2tog, k2, yo; repeat from * across to last 3 sts, k3.

Row 4: k2, p38, k2.

Row 5: k3, yo, k2, skp, k2tog, k2, yo, *k1, yo, k2, skp, k2tog, k2, yo; repeat from * across to last 4 sts, k4.

Repeat rows 2–5 for pattern until piece measures 12 in. (30.5cm), ending with row 2.

Ribbing

Row 1: k4, p2, *k2, p2; repeat from * across to last 4 sts, k4.

Row 2: k2, *p2, k2; repeat from * across.

Repeat rows 1 and 2 until ribbing measures 3 in. (7.5cm).

Bind off very loosely in ribbing.

Weave in loose ends.

Finishing

Lay knitting on the surface of a sink full of hot water. Allow to sink before draining the water, then place in a towel. Squeeze out the excess water, do not wring, and lay flat to dry. Block into shape, approximately 10½ in. (26.5cm) wide by 12 in. long (30.5cm), taking care not to stretch the ribbing.

Hook-and-Eye Tape: Once dry, cut a length of hook tape 1 in. (2.5cm) longer than your finished legwarmer.

Fold each short end of the hook tape ½ in. (13mm) to its WS and pin to WS of legwarmer.

With sewing needle and thread, whipstitch around the inside edge, working extra stitches at the top and bottom to hold the folded edge in place. For extra security, tack the tape with one or two tiny stitches in the center spot between each hook.

Repeat both steps with the eye tape on the opposite side. Check the eye tape lines up with the hook tape before sewing it in place.

Repeat for second legwarmer.

NINE OF DIAMONDS CAPELET

This project was inspired by a single, lonely playing card in the street. It was a red nine of Diamonds, and it seemed like an omen. The capelet has nine "diamond" sections and is meant for real warmth and comfort, as well as good looks. The bottoms of the diamond sections are slightly rounded, with a bit of volume built in to make them pop.

Skill level ★ ★

Yarn

- Brown Sheep Lamb's Pride Worsted Blue Blood Red #M80 [85% wool, 15% mohair; 190 yds. (173m)/113g]—4 skeins

Needles and Notions

- US size 7 16 in. circular needle and US size 8 40 in. circular needle
- ½ in. (12mm) buttons (x6) for decoration
- 1¼ in. (3cm) buttons (x2) for closure
- Tapestry needle
- Sewing needle and thread (to match yarn)

Gauge

- With larger needle, 16 sts and 22 rows = 4 in. (10cm) in St st

Size

- 17¼ in. (44cm) around neck x 68½ in. (174cm) around bottom x 16¼ in. (41.5cm) long
- One size fits most

Pattern notes

The capelet is knit flat on a circular needle to accommodate the increasing number of stitches. Knitting begins at the neck edge and works down to the hem.

It is composed of three sections, as follows:

1) six edge stitches, which are used only on left and right edges of the entire piece,

2) the diamond sections, which occur 9 times, and

3) the three stitch garter sections, which are situated between each diamond section.

With smaller circular needle, cast on 63 sts.

First Half

Rows 1–7: knit across.

Change to larger needle.

Row 8: k6, p3, *k3, p3; repeat from * 7 more times, k6.

Row 9 (RS): knit across.

Row 10: k6, p3, *k3, p3; repeat from * 7 more times, k6.

Row 11: k7, (k, yo, k) all in next st, *k5, (k, yo, k) all in next st; repeat from * 7 more times, k7—81 sts.

Row 12: k6, p5, *k3, p5; repeat from * 7 more times, k6.

Row 13: knit across.

Row 14: k6, p5, *k3, p5; repeat from * 7 more times, k6.

Row 15: k8, (k, yo, k) all in next st, *k7, (k, yo, k) all in next st; repeat from * 7 more times, k8—99 sts.

Row 16: k6, p7, *k3, p7; repeat from * 7 more times, k6.

Row 17: knit across.

Row 18: k6, p7, *k3, p7; repeat from * 7 more times, k6.

Row 19: k9, *(k, yo, k) all in next st, k9; repeat from * across—117 sts.

Row 20: k6, p9, *k3, p9; repeat from * 7 more times, k6.

Row 21: knit across.

Row 22: k6, p9, *k3, p9; repeat from * 7 more times, k6.

Row 23: k10, (k, yo, k) all in next st, *k11, (k, yo, k) all in next st; repeat from * 7 more times, k10—135 sts.

Row 24: k6, p11, *k3, p11; repeat from * 7 more times, k6.

Row 25: knit across.

Row 26: k6, p11, *k3, p11; repeat from * 7 more times, k6.

Row 27: k11, (k, yo, k) all in next st, *k13, (k, yo, k) all in next st; repeat from * 7 more times, k11—153 sts.

Row 28: k6, p13, *k3, p13; repeat from * 7 more times, k6.

Row 29: knit across.

Row 30: k6, p13, *k3, p13; repeat from * 7 more times, k6.

Row 31: k12, (k, yo, k) all in next st, *k15, (k, yo, k) all in next st; repeat from * 7 more times, k12—171 sts.

Row 32: k6, p15, *k3, p15; repeat from * 7 more times, k6.

Row 33: knit across.

Row 34: k6, p15, *k3, p15; repeat from * 7 more times, k6.

Row 35: k13, (k, yo, k) all in next st, *k17, (k, yo, k) all in next st; repeat from * 7 more times, k13—189 sts.

Get it right!

Always knit the first and last 6 stitches of each row. You may choose to slip the first stitch of each row and pull on it moderately tightly for a clean edge. This slipped stitch counts as one of the 6 edge stitches.

Row 36: k6, p17, *k3, p17; repeat from * 7 more times, k6.

Row 37: knit across.

Row 38: k6, p17, *k3, p17; repeat from * 7 more times, k6.

Row 39: k14, (k, yo, k) all in next st, *k19, (k, yo, k) all in next st; repeat from * 7 more times, k14—207 sts.

Row 40: k6, p19, *k3, p19; repeat from * 7 more times, k6.

Row 41: knit across.

Row 42: k6, p19, *k3, p19; repeat from * 7 more times, k6.

Row 43: k15, (k, yo, k) all in next st, *k21, (k, yo, k) all in next st; repeat from * 7 more times, k15—225 sts.

Row 44: k6, p21, *k3, p21; repeat from * 7 more times, k6.

Row 45: knit across.

Row 46: k6, p21, *k3, p21; repeat from * 7 more times, k6.

Row 47: k16, (k, yo, k) all in next st, *k23, (k, yo, k) all in next st; repeat from * 7 more times, k16—243 sts.

Row 48: k6, p23, *k3, p23; repeat from * 7 more times, k6.

Row 49: knit across.

Row 50: k6, p23, *k3, p23; repeat from * 7 more times, k6.

Row 51: k17, (k, yo, k) all in next st, *k25, (k, yo, k) all in next st; repeat from * 7 more times, k17—261 sts.

Row 52: k6, p25, *k3, p25; repeat from * 7 more times, k6.

Row 53: knit across.

Row 54: k6, p25, *k3, p25; repeat from * 7 more times, k6.

Row 55: k18, (k, yo, k) all in next st, *k27, (k, yo, k) all in next st; repeat from * 7 more times, k18—279 sts.

Row 56: k6, p27, *k3, p27; repeat from * 7 more times, k6.

Row 57: knit across.

Row 58: k6, p27, *k3, p27; repeat from * 7 more times, k6.

Row 59: k19, (k, yo, k) all in next st, *k29, (k, yo, k) all in next st; repeat from * 7 more times, k19—297 sts.

Row 60: k6, p29, *k3, p29; repeat from * 7 more times, k6.

Row 61: knit across.

Row 62: k6, p29, *k3, p29; repeat from * 7 more times, k6.

You have arrived at the midpoint of the capelet. The diamonds start to decrease in width, but the width of the capelet itself is maintained by eyelets outside of the diamonds. This also serves to make them pop a bit off the garter stitch background.

Second Half

Row 63: knit across.

Row 64: k6, p29, *k3, p29; repeat from * 7 more times, k6.

Row 65: knit across.

Row 66: k6, p29, *k3, p29; repeat from * 7 more times, k6.

Row 67: k6, yo, k13, dbl dec, k13, yo, *k3, yo, k13, dbl dec, k13, yo; repeat from * 7 more times, k6.

Row 68: k7, p27, *k5, p27; repeat from * 7 more times, k7.

Row 69: knit across.

Row 70: k7, p27, *k5, p27; repeat from * 7 more times, k7.

Row 71: k7, yo, k12, dbl dec, k12, yo, *k5, yo, k12, dbl dec, k12, yo; repeat from * 7 more times, k7.

Row 72: k8, p25, *k7, p25; repeat from * 7 more times, k8.

Row 73: knit across.

Row 74: k8, p25, *k7, p25; repeat from * 7 more times, k8.

Row 75: k8, yo, k11, dbl dec, k11, yo, *k7, yo, k11, dbl dec, k11, yo; repeat from * 7 more times, k8.

Row 76: *k9, p23; repeat from * 8 more times, k9.

Row 77: knit across.

Row 78: *k9, p23; repeat from * 8 more times, k9.

Row 79: *k9, yo, k10, dbl dec, k10, yo; repeat from * 8 more times, k9.

Row 80: k10, p21, *k11, p21; repeat from * 7 more times, k10.

Row 81: knit across.

Row 82: k10, p21, *k11, p21; repeat from * 7 more times, k10.

Row 83: k10, yo, k9, dbl dec, k9, yo, *k11, yo, k9, dbl dec, k9, yo; repeat from * 7 more times, k10.

Row 84: k11, p19, *k13, p19; repeat from * 7 more times, k11.

Row 85: knit across.

Row 86: k11, p19, *k13, p19; repeat from * 7 more times, k11.

Row 87: k11, yo, k8, dbl dec, k8, yo, *k13, yo, k8, dbl dec, k8, yo; repeat from * 7 more times, k11.

Row 88: k12, p17, *k15, p17; repeat from * 7 more times, k12.

Row 89: knit across.

Row 90: k12, p17, *k15, p17; repeat from * 7 more times, k12.

Row 91: k12, yo, k7, dbl dec, k7, yo, *k15, yo, k7, dbl dec, k7, yo; repeat from * 7 more times, k12.

Row 92: k13, p15, *k17, p15; repeat from * 7 more times, k13.

Row 93: knit across.

Row 94: k13, p15, *k17, p15; repeat from * 7 more times, k13.

Row 95: k13, yo, k6, dbl dec, k6, yo, *k17, yo, k6, dbl dec, k6, yo; repeat from * 7 more times, k13.

Row 96: k14, p13, *k19, p13; repeat from * 7 more times, k14.

Row 97: k14, yo, k5, dbl dec, k5, yo, *k19, yo, k5, dbl dec, k5, yo; repeat from * 7 more times, k14.

Row 98: k15, p11, *k21, p11; repeat from * 7 more times, k15.

Row 99: k15, yo, k4, dbl dec, k4, yo, *k21, yo, k4, dbl dec, k4, yo; repeat from * 7 more times, k15.

Row 100: k16, p9, *k23, p9; repeat from * 7 more times, k16.

Row 101: k16, yo, ssk 2 times, k1, k2tog 2 times, yo, *k23, yo, ssk 2 times, k1, k2tog 2 times, yo; repeat from * 7 more times, k16—279 sts.

Row 102: k17, p5, *k25, p5; repeat from * 7 more times, k17.

Row 103: k17, yo, ssk, k1, k2tog, yo, *k25, yo, ssk, k1, k2tog, yo; repeat from * 7 more times, k17.

Rows 104–111: knit across.

Bind off all sts knitwise.

Finishing

Weave in loose ends.

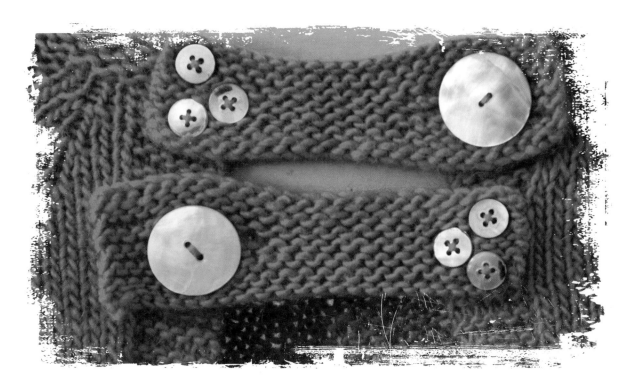

Closure Tabs (Make 2)

With smaller needle, cast on 23 sts.

Rows 1–5: knit across.

Row 6: k5, bind off next 5 sts knitwise (buttonhole made), knit across.

Row 7: knit across to bound off sts, cast on 5 sts, knit across.

Rows 8–11: knit across.

Bind off all sts knitwise.

Place the top closure tab flush with the neckline of the capelet, and attach by sewing three small buttons through both thicknesses. Add the larger button to the other side of the capelet, to line up with the buttonhole.

Add second tab in same manner, 4 rows below, reversing position of buttonhole.

Wash and block the capelet. When completely dry, steam lightly on wrong side.

RIBBED FLOWERS

These cute flower brooches make the ideal decoration. Pin them on garments, bags, scarves, hats…anything you like! They're great as gifts in their own right or you can make cards out of them by attaching them to stiff folded cardstock. Make them with leftover yarn from old projects and create them in lots of different colors to personalize whatever you're wearing.

Skill level ★

Yarn

- Sirdar Snuggly DK Daisy #259 [55% nylon, 45% acrylic; 191yds. (175m)/50g]
- Cygnet superwash DK Raspberry #2151; Bluebell #2156; Geranium #2185; Everglade #2817 [100% pure new wool, 113 yds. (104m)/50g]
- Large flower: 14 yds. (13m) MC, 6 yds. (5.5m) CC
- Small flower: 8 yds. (7.5m) MC, 4 yds. (3.5m) CC

Needles and Notions

- US size 6 (4mm) straight needles
- Pin backs
- Sewing needle and thread
- Tapestry needle
- ⅔ in. (1.5cm) button (for variation only)

Gauge

- Not important for this design

Size

- 8¼ in. (21cm) long before rolling x 1¾ in. (4.5cm) diameter when rolled up (finished flower); size varies depending on how tightly flower is rolled.

Large Flower

With MC, cast on 75 sts.

Proceed by following Chart 1 or written instructions

Row 1 (RS): k3, *p3, k3; repeat from * across.

Row 2: *p3, k3; repeat from * 9 more times (60 sts worked); turn, leaving remaining sts unworked.

Row 3: *p3, k3; repeat from * across.

Row 4: p3, *k3, p3; repeat from * 6 more times (45 sts worked); turn.

Row 5: k3, *p3, k3; repeat from * across.

Row 6: *p3, k3; repeat from * 4 more times (30 sts worked); turn.

Row 7: *p3, k3; repeat from * across.

Row 8: p3, *k3, p3; repeat from * once more (15 sts worked); turn.

Row 9: k3, *p3, k3; repeat from * across.

Row 10: change to CC, p3, *k3, p3; repeat from * across all sts.

Row 11: k3, *p3, k3; repeat from * across.

Row 12: p3, *k3, p3; repeat from * across.

Bind off all sts in ribbing; cut yarn leaving a 15 in. (38cm) tail for sewing.

Finishing

Using sewing thread, work a running stitch through flower along cast on edge.

Pull thread to gather, rolling flower into a bud shape with thin end in the center (see Fig.1).

With tail of yarn from bind off, anchor through all thicknesses.

Weave in loose ends.

Sew a pin back to the back of the flower.

Fig. 1

On RS rows, work Chart from right to left; On WS rows, work Chart from left to right.

☐	knit on RS rows; purl on WS rows
▩	unworked stitch
•	purl on RS rows; knit on WS rows

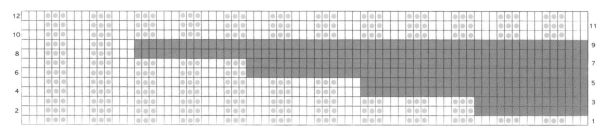

Chart 1

(Large Flower)

Small Flower

With MC, cast on 50 sts.

Proceed by following Chart 2 or written instructions

Row 1 (RS): k2, *p2, k2; repeat from * across.

Row 2: *p2, k2; repeat from * 9 more times (40 sts worked); turn, leaving remaining sts unworked.

Row 3: *p2, k2; repeat from * across.

Row 4: p2, *k2, p2; repeat from * 6 more times (30 sts worked); turn, leaving remaining sts unworked.

Row 5: k2, *p2, k2; repeat from * across.

Row 6: *p2, k2; repeat from * 4 times more (20 sts worked); turn, leaving remaining sts unworked.

Row 7: *p2, k2; repeat from * across.

Row 8: p2, *k2, p2; repeat from * once more (10 sts worked); turn, leaving remaining sts unworked.

Row 9: k2, *p2, k2; repeat from * across.

Row 10: change to CC, p2, *k2, p2; repeat from * across all sts.

Row 11: k2, *p2, k2; repeat from * across.

Bind off all sts in ribbing; cut yarn leaving a 10 in. (25cm) tail for sewing.

Finishing

Follow the steps for Finishing the large ribbed flower (see page 50).

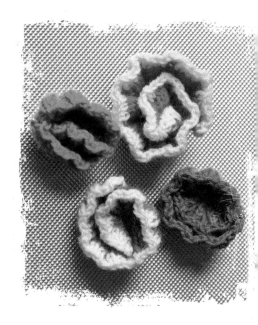

On RS rows, work Chart from right to left; On WS rows, work Chart from left to right.

☐	knit on RS rows; purl on WS rows
▩	unworked stitch
•	purl on RS rows; knit on WS rows

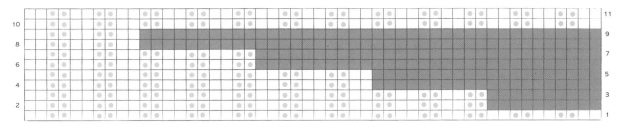

Chart 2

(Small Flower)

Variation: Petal Flower

Instead of rolling a flower from a single length of knitting, try this variation, which shows how to make a flower with individual petal shapes.

Yarn

- Sirdar Snuggly DK, Denim #326 and Putty #377 [55% nylon, 45% acrylic; 191yds. (175m)/50g]—6 yds. (5m) of each

Needles and Notions

- See Ribbed Flowers (page 48)

Size

- 4¼ in. (11cm) diameter

The center of the flower is knit first over 18 sts, then each of the 6 petals are knit using 3 sts from the center.

With first color, cast on 18 sts.

Row 1: purl across.

Row 2: knit across.

Row 3: purl across.

First Petal (uses first 3 sts)

Row 4: kfb, kfb, k1; turn, leaving remaining sts unworked—5 sts.

Row 5: purl across.

Row 6: kfb, k2, kfb, k1—7 sts.

Row 7: purl across.

Row 8: kfb, k4, kfb, k1—9 sts.

Row 9: purl across.

Row 10: kfb, k6, kfb, k1—11 sts.

Row 11: purl across.

Row 12: knit across.

Row 13: purl across.

Row 14: skp, k7, k2tog—9 sts.

Row 15: purl across.

Row 16: skp, k5, k2tog—7 sts.

Row 17: purl across.

Row 18: skp, k3, k2tog—5 sts.

Cut yarn and thread through last 5 sts; weave in tail and trim excess yarn.

Second Petal (uses next 3 sts)

With second color and working across next 3 sts on left needle, repeat rows 4–18 of First Petal. Alternating colors, continue making more petals in the same manner.

Finishing

Sew bottom ½ in. (1cm) of adjacent petals together to form a more solid flower shape; then join first and sixth petal in same manner.

Weave a length of yarn through row 3, gathering tightly.

Sew a button to the center front and a pin back to the back.

MIDNIGHT CABLE SCARF

This is a great scarf for keeping you warm but stylish, too, and is easily portable for knitters on the move. Knit for as long as you want the scarf to be. If you like to wrap a scarf around your neck several times to be as warm as possible, just knit to a longer length!

Skill level ★ ★

Yarn

- Cygnet Seriously Chunky Black #217 [100% acrylic; 52 yds. (48m)/100g]—3 skeins for long scarf, 2 skeins for short scarf

Needles and Notions

- US size 13 (9mm) straight needles
- Cable needle
- Tapestry needle

Gauge

- 16 sts and 13 rows = 4 in. (10cm) in pattern

Size

- 4 in. (10cm) wide x 5½ ft. (173cm) full length; 3 ft. (100cm) shorter length scarf

Pattern notes

Don't let a cable scare you away from this fun scarf; it's easy to make. Every WS row is stitched exactly the same way. And all of the RS rows—except one—have the same stitches.

The thick yarn used for this project makes it perfect for anyone who likes quick results since you don't need as many stitches and rows to make a good size scarf.

Cast on 16 sts.

Proceed by following Chart or written instructions.

Row 1 (RS): k3, p2, k6, p2, k3.

Row 2: p3, k2, p6, k2, p3.

Row 3: k3, p2, k6, p2, k3.

Row 4: p3, k2, p6, k2, p3.

Row 5: k3, p2, C6F, p2, k3.

Row 6: p3, k2, p6, k2, p3.

Row 7: k3, p2, k6, p2, k3.

Row 8: p3, k2, p6, k2, p3.

Row 9: k3, p2, k6, p2, k3.

Row 10: p3, k2, p6, k2, p3.

Repeat rows 5–10 for pattern until scarf measures desired length, ending with row 8.

Bind off all sts in pattern.

Finishing

Weave in loose ends.

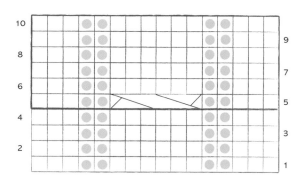

On RS rows, work Chart from right to left; On WS rows, work Chart from left to right.

☐ knit on RS rows; purl on WS rows

● purl on RS rows; knit on WS rows

⤬ C6F— slip next 3 sts onto cable needle and hold in front of work; k3 from left needle, k3 from cable needle

☐ repeat rows inside red box for pattern

LAUREN WOVEN BELT

This is a modern, knitted version of a classic leather woven belt, only made in a cruelty-free pure hemp. It holds your pants up just the same, and features a quickly memorized little cable pattern that lays perfectly flat. This belt is suitable for most cotton, hemp, bamboo, or linen yarns with no elasticity. It will be less successful if you use an animal fiber that is too soft or stretchy.

Skill level ★ ★ ★

Yarn

- Lanaknits allhemp6 Midori #035 [100% hemp; 165 yds. (150m)/100g]—2 hanks

Needles and Notions

- US size 4 (3.5mm) straight needles (metal needles are recommended for use with hemp)
- Stitch marker
- 2 in. (5cm) closed metal D Rings (x2)
- Tapestry needle

Gauge

- 22 sts and 40 rows = 4 in. (10cm) in garter stitch

Size

- 2½ in. (6cm) wide x 36 in. (91.5cm) long, or desired length, excluding D Rings

Pattern notes

Be sure to pull the first stitch tightly on non-cable rows to discourage loose edges. The resulting knit material should be somewhat stiff and sturdy.
With 2 hanks, you can make a belt up to 60 in. (1.5m) long.

Chart 1

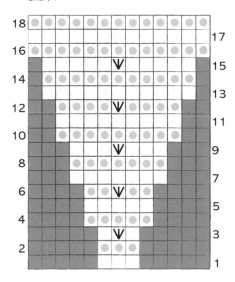

On RS rows, work Chart from right to left; On WS rows, work Chart from left to right.

☐	knit on RS rows; purl on WS rows
■	no stitch
•	purl on RS rows; knit on WS rows
V	on RS rows, (k, yo, k) all in next st; On WS rows, (p, yo, p) all in next st

Cast on 3 sts.

Proceed by following Chart 1 or written instructions.

Rows 1 and 2: knit across.

Row 3 (RS): k1, (k, yo, k) all in next st, k1—5 sts.

Rows 4 and 5: knit across.

Row 6: k2, (p, yo, p) all in next st, k2—7 sts.

Rows 7 and 8: knit across.

Row 9: k3, (k, yo, k) all in next st, k3—9 sts.

Rows 10 and 11: knit across.

Row 12: k4, (p, yo, p) all in next st, k4—11 sts.

Rows 13 and 14: knit across.

Row 15: k5, (k, yo, k) all in next st, k5—13 sts.

Rows 16–18: knit across.

Woven Cable Section

Continue by following Chart 2 or written instructions.

Row 1 (RS): [k1, m1] 3 times, k2, m1, k3, m1, k2, [m1, k1] 3 times—21 sts.

Rows 2–4: knit across.

Row 5: C6F 3 times, k3.

Row 6: k1, p1, *k2, p1; repeat from * across to last st, k1.

Row 7: knit across.

Row 8: k1, p1, *k2, p1, repeat from * across to last st, k1.

Rows 9–12: repeat rows 7 and 8 twice.

Row 13: k3, C6B 3 times.

Row 14: k1, p1, *k2, p1; repeat from * across to last st, k1.

Row 15: knit across.

Rows 16–20: repeat rows 14 and 15 twice, then repeat row 14 once more.

For a 30 in. (76cm) belt, repeat rows 5–20, 13 more times.

For a 36 in. (91.5cm) belt, repeat rows 5–20, 17 more times.

To customize the length of your belt, adjust the number of repeats of rows 5–20, ending with working row 20. Each repeat measures approximately 1½ in. (4cm).

Final section

Row 1: C6F 3 times, k3.

Rows 2–4: knit across.

Chart 2

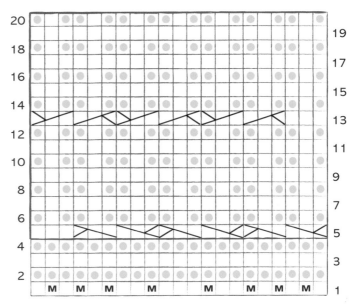

On RS rows, work Chart from right to left;
On WS rows, work Chart from left to right.

☐	knit on RS rows; purl on WS rows
M	With left needle, lift the horizontal strand between the needles and knit into the back of it.
●	knit on WS rows
⟋⟍	C6F—slip next 3 stitches onto cable needle and hold in front of work, knit 3 from left needle, knit 3 from cable needle
⟍⟋	C6B—slip next 3 stitches onto cable needle and hold in back of work, knit 3 from left needle, knit 3 from cable needle
☐	Repeat stitches enclosed in red box for desired length

Chart 3

2  1

On RS rows, work Chart from right to left; On WS rows, work Chart from left to right

☐	knit on RS rows
●	knit on WS rows
╲	ssk—slip next 2 stitches separately and knitwise to right needle. Insert left needle into the front of these 2 stitches and knit them together
∧	dbl dec—slip 2 stitches together kwise, k1, pass both slipped stitches over knit stitch (centered double decrease)

D Ring Section

Continue by following Chart 3 or written instructions.

Row 1 (RS): [k1, ssk] 3 times, dbl dec, [k1, ssk] 3 times—13 sts.

Rows 2–12: knit across. Place yarn marker at edge of last row.

Rows 13–34: knit across.

Bind off all sts. Cut yarn leaving a 12 in. (30cm) tail.

Slip the bound off edge through both D rings, folding edge to align with marked row. Whipstitch the bound off edge to the marked row.

With tapestry needle and yarn, run a seam through both layers of the belt just below the D rings to ensure a secure hold.

Finishing

Belt Loop: cast on 5 sts.

Rows 1–46: *slip 1 pwise, pull tightly, k4.

Bind off all sts, leaving a 10 in. (25cm) tail. Use tail to whipstitch cast on and bound off edges together; do not cut yarn.

Slide belt through belt loop and try on belt. Tack loop in place according to your desired fit.

Weave in loose ends.

JUTTA BERET

The Jutta Beret is a slightly slouchy, textured beret. It looks more difficult to knit than it really is. Made in a super-soft baby alpaca yarn, it is warm and lightweight, just perfect for every day wear. Enjoy!

Skill level ★ ★

Yarn

- Misti Alpaca Chunky Moss Gray Melange #M684 [100% Baby Alpaca; 108 yds. (98m)/ 100g]—2 skeins

Needles and Notions

- US size 10½ 16 in. circular needle and US size 10½ set of 5 double pointed needles
- Tapestry needle

Gauge

- 16 sts and 20 rows = 4 in. (10cm) in St st

Size

- 14 in. (35.5cm) brim circumference, unstretched

Pattern notes

The beret is composed of seven pattern repeats.

With circular needle, cast on 71 sts. Slip first cast on stitch to left needle, and knit together with last cast on stitch, being careful not to twist the sts on the needle—70 sts.

Proceed by following Chart (see page 64) or written instructions.

Rnd 1: p2, k6, *p4, k6; repeat from * around to last 2 sts, p2.

Rnd 2: p2, C6B, *p4, C6B; repeat from * around to last 2 sts, p2.

Rnds 3–5: p2, k6, *p4, k6; repeat from * around to last 2 sts, p2.

Rnd 6: p2, C6B, *p4, C6B; repeat from * around to last 2 sts, p2.

Rnds 7–10: repeat rnds 3–6.

Rnd 11: p2, (k1, yo) 5 times, k1, *p4, (k1, yo) 5 times, k1; repeat from * around to last 2 sts, p2—105 sts.

Rnd 12: p2, k11, *p4, k11; repeat from * around to last 2 sts, p2.

Rnd 13: p2, LT, k7, RT, *p4, LT, k7, RT; repeat from * around to last 2 sts, p2.

Rnd 14: p2, k1, LT, k5, RT, k1, *p4, k1, LT, k5, RT, k1; repeat from * around to last 2 sts, p2.

Rnd 15: p2, k2, LT, k3, RT, k2, *p4, k2, LT, k3, RT, k2; repeat from * around to last 2 sts, p2.

Rnd 16: p2, k3, LT, k1, RT, k3, *p4, k3, LT, k1, RT, k3; repeat from * around to last 2 sts, p2.

Rnd 17: p2, k3, RT, k1, LT, k3, *p4, k3, RT, k1, LT, k3; repeat from * around to last 2 sts, p2.

Rnd 18: p2, k2, RT, k3, LT, k2, *p4, k2, RT, k3, LT, k2; repeat from * around to last 2 sts, p2.

Rnd 19: *p2, k1, RT, k5, LT, k1, *p4, k1, RT, k5, LT, k1; repeat from * around to last 2 sts, p2.

Rnd 20: *p2, RT, k7, LT, *p4, RT, k7, LT; repeat from * around to last 2 sts, p2.

Rnd 21: *p2, LT, k7, RT, *p4, LT, k7, RT; repeat from * around to last 2 sts, p2.

Rnd 22: p2, k1, LT, k5, RT, k1, *p4, k1, LT, k5, RT, k1; repeat from * around to last 2 sts, p2.

Rnd 23: p2, k2, LT, k3, RT, k2, *p4, k2, LT, k3, RT, k2; repeat from * around to last 2 sts, p2.

Rnd 24: p2, k3, LT, k1, RT, k3, *p4, k3, LT, k1, RT, k3; repeat from * around to last 2 sts, p2.

Rnd 25: p2, k11, *p4, k11; repeat from * around to last 2 sts, p2.

Rnd 26: p2, k4, dbl dec, k4, *p4, k4, dbl dec, k4; repeat from * around to last 2 sts, p2—91 sts.

Rnd 27: p2, k9, *p4, k9; repeat from * around to last 2 sts, p2.

Rnd 28: p2, k3, dbl dec, k3, *p4, k3, dbl dec, k3; repeat from * around to last 2 sts, p2—77 sts.

Change to dpns.

Rnd 29: p2, k7, *p4, k7; repeat from * around to last 2 sts, p2.

Rnd 30: p2, k2, dbl dec, k2, *p4, k2, dbl dec, k2; repeat from * around to last 2 sts, p2—63 sts.

Rnd 31: p2, k5, *p4, k5; repeat from * around to last 2 sts, p2.

Rnd 32: p2, k1, dbl dec, k1, *p4, k1, dbl dec, k1; repeat from * around to last 2 sts, p2—49 sts.

Rnd 33: p2, k3, *p4, k3; repeat from * around to last 2 sts, p2.

Rnd 34: p2, dbl dec, *p4, dbl dec; repeat from * around to last 2 sts, p2—35 sts.

Rnd 35: p2, k1, *p4, k1; repeat from * around to last 2 sts, p2.

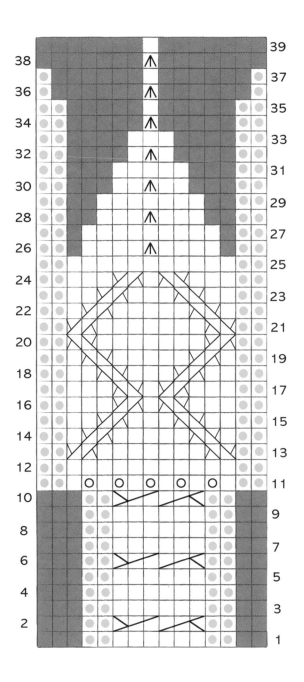

Work chart from right to left,
7 times on every round.

☐	knit every round
●	purl every round
▨	no stitch
O	yo—yarn over
⟩—⟨	C6B—slip next 3 sts onto cable needle and hold in back of work, knit 3 from left needle, knit 3 from cable needle
⟩⟨	left twist—working behind next stitch, knit the second stitch, then knit the first stitch, dropping both stitches from left needle together
⟨⟩	right twist—working in front of next stitch, knit the second stitch, then knit the first stitch, dropping both stitches from left needle together
⋀	dbl dec—slip 2 stitches together kwise, k1, pass both slipped stitches over knit stitch (centered double decrease)

Rnd 36: p1, dbl dec, *p2, dbl dec; repeat from * around to last st, p1—21 sts.

Rnd 37: *p1, k1, *p2, k1; repeat from * around to last st, p1.

Rnd 38: dbl dec around—7 sts.

Rnd 39: knit around.

Finishing

Cut yarn, leaving an 8 in. (20cm) tail. Weave tail through remaining sts, pulling tightly to close, then weave through sts again, securing on WS.

Weave in loose ends.

CHRYSALIS SHRUG

One of the fun things about knitting shrugs is that they're usually worked as one piece, shaped or not shaped, then made wearable with a few seams. This design has been reshaped a bit to move away from the usual simple tube construction while retaining warmth and practicality. Wear it loose or moderately tight, depending on the look you prefer. The modeled sample is a size medium.

Skill level ★ ★

Yarn

- Alchemy Yarns Synchronicity Passion Flower #48a [50% silk, 50% wool, 110 yds, (100m) 50g]—6 {6, 7} hanks

Needles and Notions

- US sizes 10½ and 11 24 in. circular needles
- 1½ in. (4mm) buttons (x2)
- Crochet hook: US-G/5 (4mm)
- Tapestry needle
- Sewing needle and thread (to match yarn)

Gauge

- Holding 2 strands of yarn, with larger needles, 13 sts and 17 rows = 4 in. (10cm) in St st

Size

- Small, {Medium, Large}
- Fits Chest Measurement: 35½ {39, 43} in./ 90 {99, 109} cm

Pattern notes

The shrug is knit holding two strands of yarn together. If you substitute yarn, the resulting fabric should be firm, yet drapey, neither too stiff nor too floppy. The extremely soft yet slightly elastic texture of the Synchronicity yarn inspired this pattern. It is very luxurious, light, and warm and it creates a fabric that drapes well for this shrug.

The entire shrug is knit flat, but circular needles are recomended to accommodate the large number of stitches.

Instructions are written for size small, with changes for sizes medium and large in brackets {}. If only one number is given, it applies to all sizes.

With smaller size needles and 2 strands, loosely cast on 90 {102, 114} sts.

Row 1 (RS): k4 (border), p2, *k2, p2; repeat from * across to last 4 sts, k4 (border).

Row 2: k4, p across to last 4 sts, k4.

Rows 3-7: repeat rows 1 and 2 twice, then repeat row 1 once more.

Row 8: k4, p across to last 5 sts, bind off next 3 sts (buttonhole—one st on right needle), k1.

Row 9: k2, cast on 3 sts, p1, *k2, p2; repeat from * across to last 4 sts, k4.

Row 10: k4, p across to last 4 sts, k4.

Rows 11–18: repeat rows 3–10.

Rows 19–22: repeat rows 1 and 2 twice.

Change to larger needles.

Row 23: k4, p2, k20 {24, 28}, m1right, k2, m1left, k34 {38, 42}, m1right, k2, m1left, k20 {24, 28}, p2, k4—94 {106, 118} sts.

Row 24: k4, p across to last 4 sts, k4.

Row 25: k4, p2, k21 {25, 29}, m1right, k2, m1left, k36 {40, 44}, m1right, k2, m1left, k21 {25, 29}, p2, k4—98 {110, 122} sts.

Row 26: k4, p across to last 4 sts, k4.

Row 27: k4, p2, k22 {26, 30}, m1right, k2, m1left, k38 {42, 46}, m1right, k2, m1left, k22 {26, 30}, p2, k4—102 {114, 126} sts.

Row 28: k4, p across to last 4 sts, k4.

Row 29: k4, p2, k23 {27, 31}, m1right, k2, m1left, k40 {44, 48}, m1right, k2, m1left, k23 {27, 31}, p2, k4—106 {118, 130} sts.

Row 30: k4, p across to last 4 sts, k4.

Row 31: k4, p2, k24 {28, 32}, m1right, k2, m1left, k42 {46, 50}, m1right, k2, m1left, k24 {28, 32}, p2, k4—110 {122, 134} sts.

Row 32: k4, p across to last 4 sts, k4.

Row 33: k4, p2, k25 {29, 33}, m1right, k2, m1left, k44 {48, 52}, m1right, k2, m1left, k25 {29, 33}, p2, k4—114 {126, 138} sts.

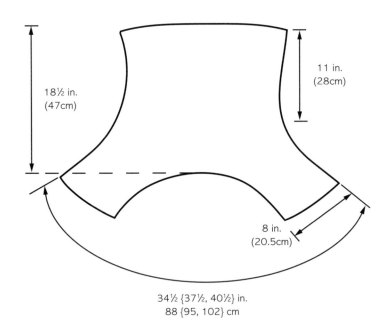

18½ in.
(47cm)

11 in.
(28cm)

8 in.
(20.5cm)

34½ {37½, 40½} in.
88 {95, 102} cm

Row 34: k4, p across to last 4 sts, k4.

Row 35: k4, p2, k26 {30, 34}, m1right, k2, m1left, k46 {50, 54}, m1right, k2, m1left, k26 {30, 34}, p2, k4—118 {130, 142} sts.

Row 36: k4, p across to last 4 sts, k4.

Row 37: k4, [p2, k2] 7 {8, 9} times, p1, m1right, k2, m1left, p1, k2, [p2, k2] 11 {12, 13} times, p1, m1right, k2, m1left, p1, [k2, p2] 7 {8, 9} times, k4 —122 {134, 146} sts.

Row 38: k4, p across to last 4 sts, k4.

Row 39: k4, p2, *k2, p2; repeat from * across to last 4 sts, k4.

Rows 40 and 41: repeat rows 38 and 39.

Row 42: bind off 31 {35, 39} sts for left front, p across to last 4 sts, k4—91 {99, 107} sts.

Row 43: bind off 31 {35, 39} sts for right front, p2, *k2, p2; repeat from * across to last st, k1—60 {64, 68} sts.

Row 44: purl across.

Row 45: k1, m1right, p2, *k2, p2; repeat from * across to last st, m1left, k1—62 {66, 70} sts.

Row 46: purl across.

Row 47: p4, k across to last 4 sts, p4.

Row 48: purl across.

Rows 49 and 50: repeat rows 47 and 48.

Row 51: p4, k2, m1right, k across to last 6 sts, m1left, k2, p4—64 {68, 72} sts.

Row 52: purl across.

Row 53: p4, k across to last 4 sts, p4.

Row 54: purl across.

Rows 55 and 56: repeat rows 53 and 54.

Rows 57–74: repeat rows 51–56, 3 times—70 {74, 78} sts.

Row 75: p4, k2, *p2, k2; repeat from * across to last 4 sts, p4.

Row 76: purl across.

Rows 77–91: repeat rows 75 and 76, 7 times, then repeat row 75 once more.

Bind off all sts purlwise.

Finishing

Weave in loose ends.

Refer to Figs. 1, 2, and 3 to fold and complete garment. Fig. 1 shows the finished piece flattened out.

Fold lower front edges to meet in the middle, lapping right front over left front (see Fig. 2).

Fold top corners down to center diagonally (see Fig. 3).

There are only two small seams now to be done! Using a single strand of yarn, join points A and C, and stitch a 3¾ in. (9.5cm) seam to create armhole. Repeat on second side, joining points B and D. (Refer to Fig. 1 for labelling of points A–D and Fig. 3 for seamed garment.)

Using a double strand of yarn, work blanket stitch evenly around each buttonhole.

Sew buttons to left front, corresponding with buttonholes.

Weave in loose ends.

Steam lightly on the inside of the shrug, taking care not to stretch the ribbing.

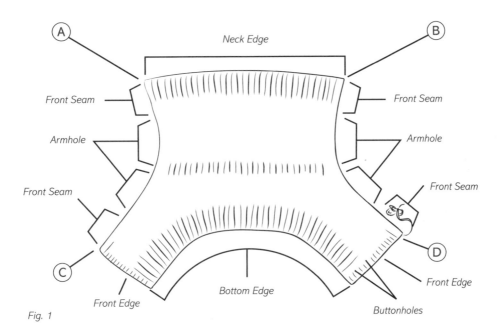

Fig. 1

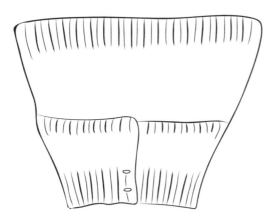

Fig. 2

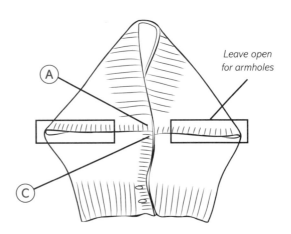

Fig. 3

DRESSING DOWN
CHAPTER 3

Full of great ideas for kicking back and relaxing, this chapter is all about the art of dressing down—without compromising on style. You'll find fabulous projects for laid-back loungewear and accessories that are as easy to make as they are to wear, but which still feel special and totally unique. The yarns chosen are soft and the pieces are comfortable to wear, perfect for weekend downtime.

The projects:

Why not rustle up a pair of Posy Striped Slippers? Choose from button strap or tie-up laces, depending on your mood. The versatile Chloe Purl or Knit Vest works as a winter underlayer or a simple cami for summer evenings. Sydney Cabled Legwarmers are incredibly versatile; pair them with old-school sneakers for on-the-go attitude, or dress them up with high heels and a skirt for the ultimate in retro glamour. The Smoke and Mirrors Smock takes its inspiration from the humble apron, but you won't want to do the chores while you wear it, and the equally stylish A Flock of Seagulls Wristlets will turn heads wherever you go. The Daisy Reversible Bag and Daisy Lined Purse are perfect for shopping as well as fun nights out with friends. Try making several in different colorways for different occasions—or turn your bag inside out for a new look. With these fantastic and individual designs, you'll be casual and comfortable yet totally stylish all at the same time.

POSY STRIPED SLIPPERS

These striped slippers are so easy to knit that they make the perfect project for beginning knitters. The button strap keeps the fit snug, but you can also choose to go for ballet-style ties if you prefer. Customise them with vintage buttons and prepare to be asked to make lots for others! The sample shown fits shoe sizes 5½–6½.

Skill level

Yarn

- Sirdar Snuggly DK, Nursery Pink #317 (Color A); Spicy Pink #350 (Color B) [55% nylon, 45% acrylic; 191yds(175m)/50g]—1 skein of each

Needles and Notions

- US size 8 (5mm) straight needles
- ½ in. (12mm) button (x2)
- Tapestry needle
- Sewing needle and thread (to match yarn)

Gauge

- Holding 2 strands of yarn, 17 sts and 32 rows = 4 in. (10cm) in garter st

Size

- Shoe size 5½–6½ {7½–8½, 9½–10½}
- Measures 6½ in. {7, 7½} in. / 16.5 {18, 19} cm from edge to edge at arch

Pattern notes

The yarn chosen for these slippers is washable, to make it easy to keep them in good condition.

You can substitute yarns in clashing colors for more contrast, or knit the slippers in one block color.

Instructions are written for size 5½–6½, with changes for sizes 7½–8½ and 9½–10½ in brackets {}. If only one number is given, it applies to all sizes.

Holding 2 strands of yarn throughout, with Color A, cast on 28 {30, 32} sts.

Rows 1 and 2: knit across; do not cut Color A. Carry unused yarn loosely along edge. Always pick up new yarn from beneath dropped yarn.

Rows 3 and 4: with Color B, knit across.

Rows 5 and 6: with Color A, knit across.

Repeat rows 3–6 for 64 {72, 80} rows.

Finishing

Cut yarn, leaving 12 in. (30cm) tail and thread yarn through remaining sts, gathering tightly. With same tail, sew ends of rows together for 2 in. (5cm) using mattress stitch.

Fold cast on edge together and sew from fold to corners to form heel.

Weave in loose ends.

Repeat for second slipper.

Button Straps (Make 2)

Cast on 20 sts.

Rows 1 and 2: knit across.

Row 3: k2, yo, k2tog (buttonhole made), k16.

Rows 4 and 5: knit across.

Bind off all sts knitwise, making sure tension remains even.

Sew one strap to inside of each slipper; sew button to outside edge on opposite side of slipper.

Variation

If you prefer the idea of pirouetting in your slippers, omit the button strap and go for ballet ties instead to keep your slippers secure.

Simply braid three 28 in. (70cm) lengths of yarn, knot the ends, and attach center of the braid to back of slipper. Repeat for second slipper.

CHLOE PURL OR KNIT VEST

This is another great project for beginning knitters. The texture and openness of the stitches is created by using 2 different size needles. Try accessorizing with a few Ribbed Flowers (see page 48). The modeled size shown is a small, and is meant to fit snugly.

Skill level

Yarn

- Sirdar Calico DK Chambray #720 [60% cotton, 40% acrylic, 172 yds. (158m)/50g]—3 skeins

Needles and Notions

- US size 6 29 in. circular needle, size 11 (8mm) and size 3 (3.25mm) straight needles
- Stitch marker
- Tapestry needle
- 2 yds. smooth scrap yarn

Gauge

- 14½ sts and 25 rows = 4 in. (10cm) in St st, knitting with largest needle and purling with smallest needle

Size

- Small {Medium, Large, X-Large}

  Finished chest measurement: 28½ {32, 36, 40} in. / 72 {81, 91.5, 101.5} cm

  Body length to underarm: 12 in. (30.5cm)

Pattern notes

The photographed sample uses the purl side of the knitting as the visible side. You could use the knit side if you prefer.

For a longer tank, use an additional skein and repeat rows 3–80 to your desired length. Three skeins will make the pattern as written for all sizes. Each additional inch (2.5cm) of length requires 7 {8, 9, 10} yards of yarn.

Instructions are written for size 5½–6½, with changes for sizes 7½–8½ and 9½–10½ in brackets {}. If only one number is given, it applies to all sizes.

Back

With smallest needle, cast on 52 {58, 65, 72} sts.

Row 1: with largest needle, knit across.

Row 2 (RS): with smallest needle, purl across.

Rows 3-80: repeat rows 1 and 2, 39 times.

Slip stitches onto scrap yarn and set aside.

Front

Work same as Back through row 80 (or to match number of rows used in Back).

Row 81: with largest needle, bind off 3 sts knitwise, knit across—49 {55, 62, 69} sts.

Row 82: with smallest needle, bind off 3 sts purlwise, purl across—46 {52, 59, 66} sts.

Row 83: with largest needle, k2tog, k across to last 2 sts, k2tog—44 {50, 57, 64} sts.

Row 84: with smallest needle, purl across.

Rows 85–92: repeat rows 83 and 84, 4 {4, 5, 5} more times—36 {42, 47, 54} sts.

Slip stitches onto scrap yarn.

Sew side seams.

Edging

With RS facing, using circular needle, and beginning at left side seam (as worn), pick up 16 {16, 18, 18} sts along left front shaping, slip 36 {42, 47, 54} sts from scrap yarn onto left needle and knit across, pick up 16 {16, 18, 18} sts along right front shaping, slip 52 {58, 65, 72} back sts from scrap yarn onto left needle and knit across, place marker to mark beginning of round—120 {132, 148, 162} sts.

Rnds 1–5: purl around.

Bind off all sts loosely pwise.

Front Straps

With RS facing, beginning at top of Front shaping, and using smallest needle, pick up 3 sts.

Knit every row for 18 in. (45cm) or to desired length.

Bind off all sts.

Repeat for second side.

Back Straps

With RS facing and beginning 15 sts from side seam, pick up 3 sts along top of the edging.

Knit every row for 18 in. (46cm) or to desired length.

Bind off all sts.

Repeat for second side.

Finishing

Weave in loose ends.

Variation

Instead of making two straps that tie up on your shoulders, you could make a longer strap for each side that goes over the shoulder and attaches to the back of the vest—either straight or crossed over each other. First measure how long the straps need to be, then knit to your desired length. Measure again to check length before binding off. Weave ends to back of vest.

SYDNEY CABLED LEGWARMERS

Always a necessity for dancers, from ballet to disco, the recent resurgence of legwarmers cements their status as an accessory staple in any fashionable and practical woman's wardrobe. Sydney features an original cable and twisted dividers that are fun to knit. The results look much more complicated than they are to make.

Skill level ★ ★

Yarn

- Karabella Merino Superwash #12947 dark rose [100% merino wool; 91 yds. (83m)/50g]—5 balls

Needles and Notions

- US size 7 (4.5mm) set of 5 double pointed needles and US size 8 (5mm) set of 5 double pointed needles
- Cable needle
- Tapestry needle

Gauge

- With larger size needles, 16 sts and 22 rows = 4 in. (10cm) in St st

Size

- 11 in. (28cm) circumference x 15¼ in. (38.5cm) long

Pattern notes

These legwarmers are knit from the top down, and the top ribbing is longer than the bottom ribbing.

The chosen yarn, Karabella, is very elastic and soft, as well as machine washable. If you substitute yarn, try to find one that has good elasticity.

Top Ribbing

Using smaller dpns, cast on 60 sts (15 sts per needle). Work ribbing as explained here or follow Chart (see page 83). One complete pattern will be worked on each needle. Join, being careful not to twist.

Rnd 1 (RS): *p1, k2; repeat from * around.

Rnd 2: *p1, LT; repeat from * around.

Rnds 3–18: repeat rnds 1 and 2, 8 times.

Cable Section

Change to larger dpns. Continue working Chart rows or follow rnd-by-rnd instructions below.

Rnd 19: *p1, k2, p1, m1, k2, m1, k4, m1, k2, m1, p1, k2; repeat from * around—76 sts (19 sts on each needle).

Rnd 20: *p1, LT, p1, k12, p1, LT; repeat from * around.

Rnd 21: *p1, k2, p1, C4B, C8F, p1, k2; repeat from * around.

Rnd 22: *p1, LT, p1, k12, p1, LT; repeat from * around.

Rnd 23: *p1, k2, p1, k12, p1, k2; repeat from * around.

Rnd 24: *p1, LT, p1, k12, p1, LT; repeat from * around.

Rnd 25: *p1, k2, p1, C4B, k8, p1, k2; repeat from * around.

Rnd 26: *p1, LT, p1, k12, p1, LT; repeat from * around.

Rnd 27: *p1, k2, p1, k12, p1, k2; repeat from * around.

Rnd 28: *p1, LT, p1, k12, p1, LT; repeat from * around.

Rnd 29: *p1, k2, p1, C8B, C4F, p1, k2; repeat from * around.

Rnd 30: *p1, LT, p1, k12, p1, LT; repeat from * around.

Rnd 31: *p1, k2, p1, k12, p1, k2; repeat from * around.

Rnd 32: *p1, LT, p1, k12, p1, LT; repeat from * around.

Rnd 33: *p1, k2, p1, k8, C4F, p1, k2; repeat from * around.

Rnd 34: *p1, LT, p1, k12, p1, LT; repeat from * around.

Rnd 35: *p1, k2, p1, k12, p1, k2; repeat from * around.

Rnd 36: *p1, LT, p1, k12, p1, LT; repeat from * around.

Rnd 37–117: repeat rnds 21–36, 5 times, then repeat rnd 21 once more.

Bottom Ribbing

Change to smaller dpns. Continue working Chart rows or follow rnd-by-rnd instructions below.

Rnd 118: *p1, LT, p1, [ssk, k1] 4 times, p1, LT; repeat from * around—60 sts.

Rnd 119: *p1, k2; repeat from * around.

Rnd 120: *p1, LT; repeat from * around.

Rnds 121–126: repeat rnds 119 and 120, 3 times.

Bind off all sts in pattern.

Repeat for second legwarmer.

Finishing

Weave in loose ends.

Turn WS out and steam lightly on the inside of legwarmers, making sure not to stretch. They're ready to wear!

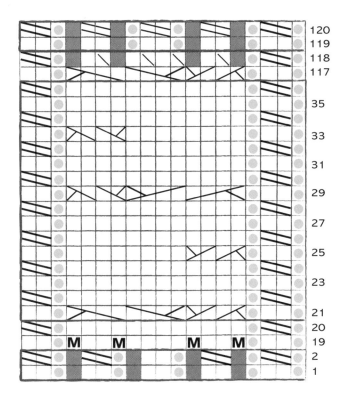

	120
	119
	118
	117
	35
	33
	31
	29
	27
	25
	23
	21
	20
	19
	2
	1

Work chart from right to left on every round

▨	no stitch
☐	knit every round
●	purl every round
╲	ssk—slip next 2 stitches separately and knitwise to right needle. Insert left needle into the front of these 2 stitches and knit them together
M	with left needle, lift the horizontal strand between the needles and knit into the back of it
═	left twist (LT)—skip first stitch and knit into the back of the second stitich, then knit the first stitch from the front and slide both stitches off the left needle
╲╱╲	C4B—slip next 2 sts onto cable needle and hold in back of work, knit 2 from left needle, knit 2 from cable needle
╱╲╱	C4F—slip next 2 sts onto cable needle and hold in front of work, knit 2 from left needle, knit 2 from cable needle
╱╲╲	C8F—slip next 4 sts onto cable needle and hold in front of work, knit 4 from left needle, knit 4 from cable needle
╲╱╱	C8B—slip next 4 sts onto cable needle and hold in back of work, knit 4 from left needle, knit 4 from cable needle
☐	work instructions enclosed in box 4 times

DAISY LINED PURSE

You can never have too many purses—one for day or for night, one for carrying cash or makeup, and another to store jewelry. This neat button-closed purse is easy to knit and ideal for using up leftover bits of yarn. It is lined to keep it in shape. Experiment with yarns and fabrics to create the perfect purse for any occasion.

Skill level ★

Yarn

- Sirdar Snuggly DK, Denim #326 (Color A), Spicy Pink #0350 (Color B), Daisy #259 (Color C) [55% nylon, 45% acrylic; 191yds. (175m)/50g]—1 skein of Denim, 7 yds. (6.5m) of Spicy Pink, 3 yds. (2.75m) of Daisy

Needles and Notions

- US size 6 (4mm) straight needles
- Crochet hook: US-F/5 (3.75mm)
- Fabric for lining, at least 11 in. (28cm) x 6 in. (15cm)
- Sewing needle and thread (to match Denim yarn)
- 1 in. (2.5cm) button
- Tapestry needle

Gauge

- 23½ sts and 29 rows = 4 in. (10cm) in St st

Size

- 5¼ in. (13.5cm) wide x 4¼ in. (11cm) high folded

Pattern notes

The purse lining is important because it adds stability and stops sharper objects poking through the stitches. Attaching the lining right at the end, after the purse is folded and sewn up, will hide any loose ends and keep the inside neat and tidy.

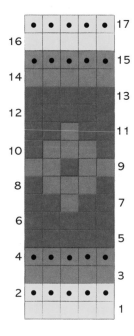

Work Chart 6 times on every row, working from right to left on RS rows and left to right on WS rows.

Knit on RS rows, purl on WS rows, in color indicated.

With Color A, cast on 30 sts.

Rows 1–31: beginning with a knit row, work in St st for 31 rows.

Row 32 (folding ridge): knit across.

Rows 33–63: beginning with a knit row, work in St st for 31 rows.

Row 64 (folding ridge): knit across.

Rows 65–70: beginning with a knit row, work in St st for 6 rows.

Row 71: with Color C, knit across (first row of Chart); cut Color C.

Row 72: with Color B, purl across (second row of Chart); do not cut Color B. Carry yarn loosely along edge of piece.

Rows 73–83: continue to work in St st, referring to chart for color changes; cut Color B and Color A.

Row 84: with Color C, knit across.

Bind off all sts purlwise.

Finishing

Fold purse along folding ridges and neatly sew side seams.

Take lining fabric and hem each edge so piece measures 5½ in. x 10½ in. (14cm x 27cm),
leaving a seam allowance of ½ in. (1cm) on each side.

Fold fabric in same manner as purse, with the top flap measuring 2½ in. (6cm). Stitch side edges of fabric. Slip lining inside the knitted purse and neatly sew edges of lining to purse.

Using crochet hook, join Color A with slip stitch ½ in. (1cm) to right of center of bound off edge, chain a short length for button loop; join with slip stitch ½ in. (1cm) to left of center, fasten off.

Weave in loose ends.

Sew button to purse opposite button loop.

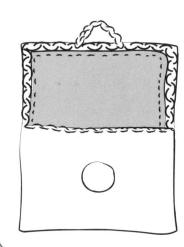

DAISY REVERSIBLE BAG

This bag complements the Daisy Lined Purse perfectly. The pattern is an extension of the one on the purse and uses the same colors and yarn. But it is also reversible. Show off the bold pattern or turn it inside out and showcase the blended colors of the reverse side.

Skill level ★

Yarn

- Sirdar Snuggly DK, Spicy Pink #0350 (Color A), Daisy #259 (Color B), Denim #326 (Color C) [55% nylon, 45% acrylic; 191yds (175m)/50g] —2 skeins of Spicy Pink, 1 skein each of Daisy and Denim

Needles and Notions

- US size 6 (4mm) straight needles
- Tapestry needle

Gauge

- 23½ sts and 29 rows = 4 in. (10cm) in St st

Size

- 13½ in. (34cm) wide x 11½ in. (29.5cm) high

Pattern notes

If you want to be able to use the reverse side, make sure to sew the bag up carefully so that your floats on the reverse of the stitches are neat. See Color Pattern Knitting—Fair Isle (see page 20) for details.

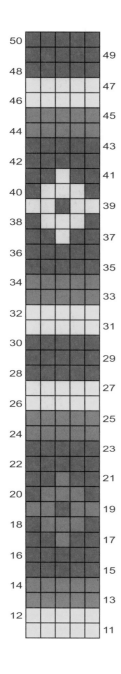

With Color C, cast on 80 sts.

Rows 1–10: beginning with a knit row, work in St st.

Begin following Chart.

Row 11 (RS): with Color B, knit across.

Row 12: purl across.

Continue to work in St st, following Chart for color pattern. Work rows 13–50 of Chart, then work rows 11–50 twice, then work rows 11–27 once more.

Last 10 rows: with Color C and beginning with a purl row, work 10 rows in St st.

Bind off all sts purlwise.

Strap

With 2 strands of Color C, cast on 6 sts.

Knit for 100 rows (50 ridges).

Bind off all sts knitwise.

Work Chart 16 times on every row, working from right to left on RS rows and left to right on WS rows.

Knit on RS rows, purl on WS rows, in color indicated.

Ribbed Trim

With Color A, cast on 120 sts.

Rows 1–14: *k2, p2; repeat from * across.

Row 15: k2 *p2, k2; repeat from * 11 times more, bind off next 8 sts, work in established ribbing across next 51 sts (52 sts after last bind off), bind off next 8 sts, work in established ribbing across remaining sts.

Row 16: *work in established ribbing across to bound off sts, cast on 8 sts; repeat from * once more, work in established ribbing across.

Rows 17–30: *k2, p2; repeat from * across.

Bind off all sts in ribbing.

Finishing

Fold bag in half with right sides together and neatly weave side edges.

Fold right sides of short edges of ribbed trim together to form a ring and weave seam.

Whipstitch one end of strap to top side edge of bag. Slip strap through holes in ribbed trim (see Fig. 1).

Fig. 1

Sew second end of strap to opposite side of bag.

Neatly whipstitch ribbed trim to top of bag (see Fig. 2).

Weave in loose ends.

Fig. 2

A FLOCK OF SEAGULLS WRISTLETS

These wristlets were inspired by a vague memory of a 1980s album cover. Visuals can stick with us indefinitely, hiding in the recesses of our minds and resurfacing when least expected. Be careful what you look at, because it may reappear when you least expect it!

Skill level ★ ★ ★

Yarn

- Lavish Fibres Alpaca Electric Blue (Color A) and Cream (Color B) [100% superfine alpaca, 219 yds. (200m)/50g]—one ball of each color

Needles and Notions

- US size 2 (2.75mm) straight needles
- Crochet hook: US-B/1 (2.25mm)
- ½ in. (12mm) buttons (x8)
- Tapestry needle
- Sewing needle and thread

Gauge

- 18 sts and 36 rows = 2 in. (5cm) in garter stitch

Size

- 3½ in. x 9 in. (9cm x 23cm)

Pattern notes

These wristlets use the mosaic knitting technique. You knit two rows with one color, while slipping the stitches of the opposite color according to a chart. You then knit two rows with the color of the previously slipped stitches, again slipping stitches according to the chart, this time slipping the stitches of the first color. The result is a center geometric design with striped borders.

Notice that the pattern sections on each wristlet look slightly different. The first color you use for the interior section of each row is considered the background, and will be slightly more prominent. If you follow the charts exactly, yours will look slightly different, too.

Left Wristlet

Note: Pull yarn tightly when changing colors to keep edge flat.

With Color B, cast on 32 sts.

Rows 1 (RS) and 2: knit across.

Rows 3 and 4: with Color A, knit across.

Rows 5 and 6: with Color B, knit across.

Rows 7–10: repeat rows 3–6.

Begin following Left Wristlet Chart as follows:

Row 11: with Color A, k4 (border), work Row 11 of Chart 3 times from right to left across center 24 sts as follows: *(k2, slip 2 pwise wyib) twice; repeat from * 2 times more, k4 (border).

Row 12: k4, work same row of chart 3 times from left to right across center 24 sts as follows: *(slip 2 pwise wyif, k2) twice; repeat from * 2 times more, k4.

Row 13: with Color B, k4, work next row of Chart 3 times from right to left across center 24 sts as follows: *(slip 2 pwise wyib, k2) twice; repeat from * 2 times more, k4.

Left Wristlet

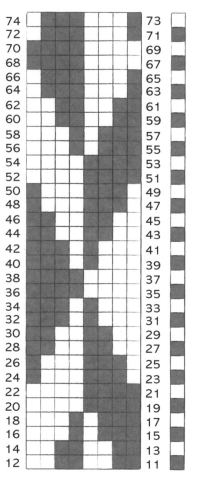

Work Chart rows 11–74, twice; then work rows 11–14 once more.

On RS rows, follow chart from right to left; On WS rows, follow Chart from left to right.

Always work row in color indicated in color bar to the right of Chart.

Carry unused yarn loosely along edge. Always pick up new yarn from beneath dropped yarn.

On odd numbered rows (RS), knit all sts indicated by the current color and slip all other stitches with the working yarn held in back.

The second, even-numbered, row (WS) of a color is worked as a mirror image of the first row—knit all knitted stitches and slip all slipped sts while holding the working yarn in front of the work.

Row 14: k4, work same row of chart 3 times from left to right across center 24 sts as follows: *(k2, slip 2 pwise wyif) twice; repeat from * 2 times more, k4.

Row 15: with Color A, k4, work next row of chart 3 times from right to left across center 24 sts, k4.

Row 16: k4, work same row of chart from left to right across center 24 sts, k4.

Row 17: with Color B, k4, work next row of chart from right to left across center 24 sts, k4.

Row 18: k4, work same row of chart from left to right across center 24 sts, k4.

Rows 19–150: complete Chart rows 11–74 twice, then rows 11–14 once more.

Rows 151 and 152: with Color A, knit across.

Rows 153 and 154: with Color B, knit across.

Row 155: with Color A, k4, *bind off next 4 sts, k2 (3 sts on needle after bind off); repeat from * across—4 buttonholes.

Row 156: *k3, cast on 4 sts; repeat from * across to last 4 sts, k4.

Rows 157 and 158: with Color B, knit across.

Rows 159 and 160: with Color A, knit across; at end of row 160, cut Color A.

Rows 161 and 162: with Color B, knit across.

With Color B, bind off all sts.

Right Wristlet

With Color B, cast on 32 sts.

Rows 1 and 2: knit across.

Rows 3 and 4: with Color A, knit across.

Rows 5 and 6: with Color B, knit across.

Row 7: with Color A, k4, *bind off next 4 sts, k2 (3 sts on needle after bind off); repeat from * across—4 buttonholes.

Row 8: *k3, cast on 4 sts; repeat from * across to last 4 sts, k4.

Rows 9 and 10: with Color B, knit across.

Rows 11 and 12: with Color A, knit across.

Begin following Right Wristlet Chart (see page 97) as follows:

Row 13: with Color B, k4 (border), work row 13 of Chart 3 times from right to left across center 24 sts as follows: *k4, slip 4 pwise wyib; repeat from * 2 times more, k4 (border).

Row 14: k4, work same row of Chart 3 times from left to right across center 24 sts as follows: *slip 4 pwise wyif, k4; repeat from * 2 times more, k4.

Row 15: with Color A, k4, work next row of Chart 3 times from right to left across center 24 sts as follows: *slip 4 pwise wyib, k4; repeat from * 2 times more, k4.

Row 16: k4, work same row of Chart 3 times from left to right across center 24 sts as follows: *k4, slip 4 pwise wyif; repeat from * 2 times more, k4 (border).

Row 17: with Color B, k4, work next row of chart 3 times from right to left across center 24 sts, k4.

Row 18: k4, work same row of Chart from left to right across center 24 sts, k4.

Row 19: with Color A, k4, work next row of Chart from right to left across center 24 sts, k4.

Row 20: k4, work same row of Chart from left to right across center 24 sts, k4.

Rows 21–152: complete Chart rows 13–76 twice, then rows 13–16 once more.

Rows 153 and 154: with Color B, knit across.

Rows 155 and 156: with Color A, knit across.

Rows 157 and 158: with Color B, knit across.

Rows 159–162: repeat rows 155–158; at end of row 160, cut Color A.

With Color B, bind off all sts.

Finishing—Both Wristlets

Weave in loose ends.

With right side facing, and using crochet hook, join yarn with slip st in bottom left corner; working from left to right, crab stitch in end of each Color A row across.

Do not work crab stitch in the edge with color changes.

Steam heavily on WS side of work, or wash and block flat. Sew on four buttons to correspond to buttonholes on each wristlet.

The color change edge is worn closest to the wrist.

Right Wristlet

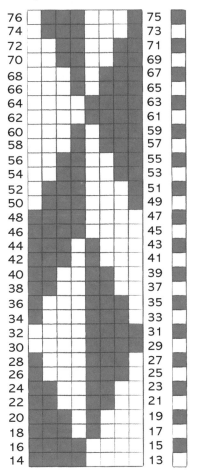

Work Chart rows 13–76, twice; then repeat rows 13–16 once more.

On RS rows, follow Chart from right to left; On WS rows, follow chart from left to right.

Always work row in color indicated in color bar to right of Chart.

Carry unused yarn loosely along edge. Always pick up new yarn from beneath dropped yarn.

On odd numbered rows (RS), knit all sts indicated by the current color and slip all other stitches with the yarn held in back.

The second, even-numbered, row (WS) of a color is worked as a mirror image of the first row—knit all knitted stitches and slip all slipped sts holding the yarn in front of the work.

SMOKE AND MIRRORS SMOCK

This piece can be made either in several small pieces or as one, larger whole. Its name refers to both the color and the slightly sneaky revelation of an open back. Comforting as a woolen overlay in colder months, or as a lightweight warm weather garment if knit in cotton.

Skill level ★ ★

Yarn

- Cascade Eco Wool #7097 blue-gray [100% natural Peruvian wool, 468 yds (435m)/250g]—1 hank (Suggested cotton yarn substitution: Blue Sky Alpacas Dyed Cotton [100% organic]—4 hanks)

Needles and Notions

- US size 9 24 in. circular needle
- 2–3 yards elastic thread
- Tapestry needle
- 1⅛ in. (3cm) button
- Sewing needle and thread (to match yarn)

Gauge

- 16 sts and 20 rows = 4 in. (10cm) in St st

Size

- Small {Medium, Large}
- Fits rib cage measurement: 25–28 {29–32, 33–36} in. / 63.5–71 {73.5–81, 84–91.5} cm

Pattern notes

The seven narrow gores making up the body of the garment are knit separately and seamed together at the end. To knit the body in one continuous piece, multiply the gore pattern by seven and repeat it across the row.

A four-stitch row lace pattern called "Feather and Fan" creates the scalloped hem and features gentle internal decreases that will meet the bodice pieces just below the bust.

The bodice is made up of two cups and crossing back straps that are seamed to the body to complete the garment. Elastic thread can be woven into the bound off edge of each strap for comfort and to preserve the shape and add stability.

A circular needle is recommended to accommodate the large number of stitches needed for the bodice straps, but the pattern can be worked on straight needles.

Gore (Make 7)

Cast on 20 sts.

Row 1 (RS): knit across.

Row 2: purl across.

Row 3: k1, k2tog 3 times, (yo, k1) 6 times, k2tog 3 times, k1.

Row 4: knit across.

Rows 5–56 {60, 64}: repeat rows 1–4, 13 {14, 15} times (14 {15, 16} ridges on RS).

Top Shaping:

Row 1: knit across.

Row 2: purl across.

Row 3 (Decrease row): k1, k2tog 3 times, (k1 yo) 4 times, k2, k2tog 3 times, k1—18 sts.

Row 4: knit across.

Size Large only: bind off all sts loosely knitwise.

Row 5: knit across.

Row 6: purl across.

Row 7 (Decrease row): k1, k2tog 3 times, (yo, k1) 4 times, k2tog 3 times, k1—16 sts.

Row 8: knit across.

Size Medium only: bind off all sts loosely knitwise.

Row 9: knit across.

Row 10: purl across.

Row 11: k2tog 3 times, (yo, k1) 4 times, k2tog 3 times— 14 sts.

Row 12: knit across.

Bind off all sts loosely knitwise.

All sizes: sew gores together to form A-line apron (see Fig. 1).

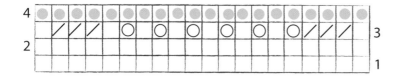

On RS rows, work chart from right to left; On WS rows, work chart from left to right.

	knit on RS rows; purl on WS rows
/	k2tog–knit next 2 sts together
◯	yarn over
●	knit on WS rows

Bodice

The bodice is made of two flat pieces that, when seamed, become a three-dimensional, lingerie-inspired, bra top.

Left Side:

Cast on 92 {98, 106} sts.

Rows 1–7: *k1, p1; repeat from * across.

Row 8 (RS): bind off first 48 sts loosely in ribbing (one st remains on right needle), p1, *k1, p1; repeat from * 13 more times (30 sts on right needle), bind off last 14 {20, 28} sts loosely in ribbing; cut yarn.

Rows 9–26: with WS facing, rejoin yarn and work in k1, p1 ribbing over center 30 sts for 18 rows.

Row 27: Bind off 12 sts, p1, *k1, p1; repeat from * across— 18 sts.

Rows 28–37: *k1, p1; repeat from * across.

Bind off all sts loosely in ribbing.

Right Side:

The right side is the mirror image of the left side with additional stitches in back for button tab with eyelet hole.

Cast on 97 {103, 111} sts.

Row 1: p1, *k1, p1; repeat from * across.

Row 2 (RS): k1, *p1, k1; repeat from * across.

Row 3: p1, *k1, p1; repeat from * across.

Row 4: *k1, p1; repeat from * across to last 3 stitches, yo, k2tog, k1.

Rows 5–7: repeat rows 1–3.

Row 8 (RS): bind off first 19 {25, 33} sts loosely in ribbing (one st remains on right needle, k1, *p1, k1; repeat from * 13 more times (30 sts on right needle), bind off last 48 sts loosely in ribbing; cut yarn.

Rows 9–25: with WS facing, rejoin yarn and work in k1, p1 ribbing for 18 rows.

Row 26: bind off 12 sts, p1, *k1, p1; repeat from * across— 18 sts.

Rows 27–37: *k1, p1; repeat from * across.

Bind off all sts loosely in ribbing.

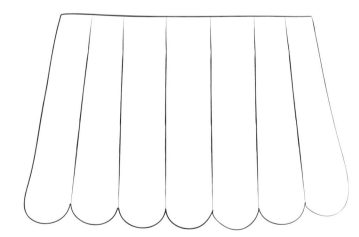

Fig. 1

Finishing

Each cup has a long edge with what appears to be a stair step in center (see top part of Fig. 2). The bust dart is made by weaving together the notch in the stair step, resulting in a slight pyramid shape (see bottom part of Fig. 2). Cast on edge fits around underarm, over shoulder, and across back.

Weave each dart seam.

Lay right and left bodice sides in front of you with RS facing and shorter bound off edges to outside.

Locate center of the apron along bound off edge (98 {112, 126} sts total, with 49 {56, 63} sts on each side of center).

Pin each side of bodice to the top of apron, matching at center front and keeping 5 sts of right back free for buttonhole overlap.

Weave each side of bodice from center front to center back.

Using sewing needle and thread, sew button to back of left bodice.

In order to gauge proper placement of back straps, try on smock and pin straps in position, adjusting as necessary

Using tapestry needle, sew straps to back edge of body.

If desired, weave elastic thread through WS of button tab and bound off edge along back right panel, side of cup and along strap. Using sewing needle and thread, secure elastic. Repeat for left side.

Immerse entire garment in tub of warm water. Allow piece to sink, then gently press out excess water. Use a towel to absorb as much additional moisture as possible. Dry flat, pinning into shape.

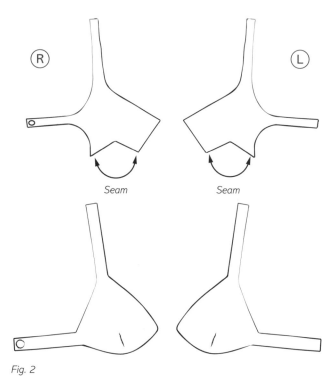

Fig. 2

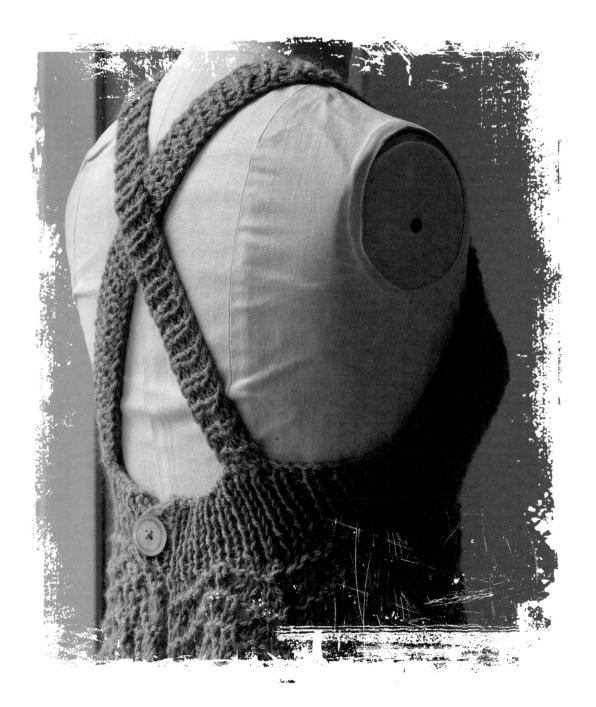

DRESSING WARM
CHAPTER 4

Each of the projects in this chapter is designed to keep you warm and stylish on cold winter days, no matter where you are or what you're doing, whether you're looking to whip up something simple or keen to try a more advanced project. Scarves are often a good place for beginning knitters to start because you don't have to worry about shaping. They are ideal for getting used to a particular stitch or pattern, whether cables, intarsia knitting, or just plain knit and purl stitches. Once you've knit the same stitch over and over again, you'll be sure to have mastered it. Then you will have the confidence to move on to more challenging pieces.

Several of the projects use similar techniques, so feel free to create your own matching set by knitting different projects in the same yarn. Or, keep them mismatched and clashing for great contrast. Whatever works for you!

The projects:

Why not channel your inner afghan with the Retro Angle Scarf, or dream of snow-covered mountains while you create your own Nordic Snowflake set of Hat and Mittens. The stylish Ha'Penny Loop Cowl and the Ellen Mitered Earwarmer will make you wish it was winter all year round, while the Chunky Check Collar is beautifully simple yet totally practical. The Taproot Sash is an elegant obi-style belt that provides added warmth as well as giving you a great silhouette. And if you're still searching for the perfect headgear, then fear not: the Tepee Slouch Hat will turn heads at the same time as keeping you toasty, while the funky Cozy Cable Hat has a pompom that's almost as big as the hat itself.

CHUNKY CHECK COLLAR

You will love this collar. Not only is it easy to knit, but also very easy to wear. Knit it in any color or pattern to match any top. The simple knit and purl check pattern is ideal for beginning knitters and the thick wool knits up quickly. Have fun with this project, experiment with stitch patterns and colors, and create a collar for every occasion.

Skill level ★

Yarn

- Sirdar Big Softie Super Chunky Meringue #330 [51% wool, 49% acrylic, 49yds. (45m)/50g]—2 skeins

Needles and Notions

- US size 13 (9mm) straight needles or 16 in. circular needle
- Tapestry needle

Gauge

- 12 sts and 14 rows = 4 in. (10cm) in pattern

Size

- 16 in. (41cm) circumference x 7 in. (18cm) high

Pattern notes

This collar can be knitted on a circular needle, which would keep you from having to sew up the back and would give you a neater finish. Using a circular needle, cast on 48 sts; being careful not to twist sts, join to work in the rnd. Place marker to mark the beginning of the rnd.

Rnds 1–4: *k2, p2; repeat from * around.

Rnds 5–8: *p2, k2; repeat from * around.

Repeat rnds 1–8 twice or until desired length, ending with rnd 4 or rnd 8.

Bind off all sts in pattern.

Cast on 48 sts.

Rows 1–4: *k2, p2; repeat from * across.

Rows 5–8: *p2, k2; repeat from * across.

Repeat rows 1–8 twice or until desired length, ending with row 4 or row 8.

Bind off all sts knitwise.

Finishing

Weave short edges together.

Weave in loose ends.

With WS facing out, steam lightly.

RETRO ANGLE SCARF

This scarf is reminiscent of an afghan from the seventies... only without the shock! Back then, bright acrylic yarns were new and modern, but did no one notice how terrible they felt to wear? Now you can steal the color cues of our fore-knitters, without all the itching pain. Go ahead, channel your inner afghan...

Skill level ★

Yarn

- Manos del Uruguay Wool Clasica Cerise #47 (Color A), Hibiscus #69 (Color B), Cherry #48 (Color C), Bing Cherry #300M (Color D) [100% wool; 138 yds. (125m)/100g]—1 hank of each color

Needles and Notions

- US size 10½ (6.5mm) straight needles
- Crochet hook: US-K/10½ (6.5mm)
- Tapestry needle

Gauge

- 12 sts and 16 rows = 4 in. (10cm) in St st

Size

- 10 in. (25.5cm) x 112 in. (2.8m)

Pattern notes

This pattern is reversible, so your scarf will look fine on either side. It's written using 4 different colors with subtle color shifts but it can easily be worked in one color or with a different combination.

On many of the rows you work an increase and a decrease. These adjustments create the angled effect. The number of stitches you have on your needle at the end of every row will always be the same.

Adding a long fringe is completely optional, but it definitely adds to the retro vibe!

With color A, cast on 30 sts.

Row 1 (RS): purl across.

Row 2: kfb, k to last stitch, skp.

Row 3: purl across.

Row 4: kfb, k to last stitch, skp.

Row 5: knit across.

Row 6: pfb, p to last stitch, skp.

Row 7: knit across.

Row 8: pfb, p to last stitch, skp.

Rows 9–24: repeat rows 1–8 twice—6 ridges.

Rows 25–48: with color B, repeat rows 1–8, 3 times.

Rows 49–72: with color C, repeat rows 1–8, 3 times.

Rows 73–104: with color D, repeat rows 1–8, 4 times.

Rows 105–128: with color C, repeat rows 1–8, 3 times.

Rows 129–152: with color B, repeat rows 1–8, 3 times.

Rows 153–176: with color A, repeat rows 1–8, 3 times.

Bind off all sts purlwise.

Finishing

Weave in loose ends.

Fringe (Optional)

Cut a piece of cardboard 5 in. (12.5cm) wide and ½ in. (12 mm) longer than you want your finished fringe to be.

Wind the remaining yarn loosely and evenly lengthwise around the cardboard until the card is filled, then cut across one end.

Hold together 5 strands of yarn.

Fold strands in half.

Using a crochet hook, draw the folded end up through a corner stitch and pull loose ends through the folded end.

Draw the knot up tightly. Repeat 9 times more, evenly spaced across end of scarf, cutting more strands (as explained above) as needed. Repeat across second end.

Steam lightly and trim ends.

TEPEE SLOUCH HAT

Creative folding and finishing of the edge on the top of this hat results in a 3D asterisk shape. Try working the top closure in a different color for more emphasis! You can make Tepee as a cowl if you prefer—the stitch pattern will give the piece a dramatic sawtooth edge.

Skill level ★ ★

Yarn

- Blue Sky Alpacas Melange Orange Zest #801 and Salsa #806 [100% baby alpaca; 110 yds. (100m)/50g]—2 hanks of each color
- Small amount of smooth waste yarn for cast on

Needles and Notions

- US size 9 16 in. circular needle or straight needles and US size 8 16 in. circular needle
- Crochet hook: US-G/6 (4mm)
- Tapestry needle

Gauge

- Holding 2 strands of yarn, with larger needles, 16 sts and 20 rows = 4 in. (10cm) in St st

Size

- 19 in. (48.5cm) circumference x 9 in. (23cm) high

Pattern notes

Tepee is knit using two strands held together, one of each color. The sample shown was made with two shades of orange to give extra visual depth. Whether you make a hat or a cowl, the piece is knit flat, then the cast on edge and the last row are grafted together. The top of the hat is finished with single crochet and crab stitch.

In this pattern, Make 1 (M1) is done by lifting the horizontal strand between the needles and knitting into the back of it.

If you want to make a longer cowl (a wider circumference), repeat rows 1–18 of the pattern until you've reached your desired depth. If you are using the recommended yarn, you will have enough to add four more chart repeats, plus the last 2 rows to finish the final strip.

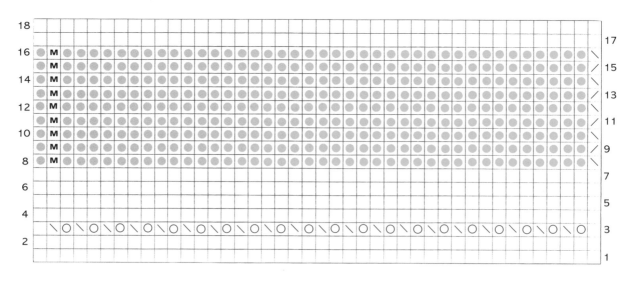

With waste yarn and larger size needle(s), cast on 42 sts and knit one row.

Change to a double strand of your project yarn (one strand of each color held together).

Begin following row 1 of Chart or follow written instructions. If following Chart, work rows 1–18, five times, then work rows 91 and 92 of written instructions.

Row 1 (RS): knit across.

Row 2: purl across.

Row 3: k1, * yo, ssk; repeat from * across to last st, k1.

Row 4: purl across.

Row 5: knit across.

Row 6: purl across.

Row 7: knit across.

Row 8: k1, m1, k39, ssk.

Row 9: p2tog, p39, m1, p1.

Row 10: k1, m1, k39, ssk.

Rows 11–16: repeat rows 9 and 10, 3 times.

Row 17: knit across.

Row 18: purl across.

Rows 19–90: repeat rows 1–18, 4 times.

Row 91: knit across.

Row 92: purl across.

Cut yarn leaving a 4 ft. (122cm) tail. The tail will be used to graft the cast on edge and last row together.

On RS rows, work chart from right to left; On WS rows, work chart from left to right.

▢	knit on RS rows; purl on WS rows
●	purl on RS rows; knit on WS rows
○	yo—yarn over
\	ssk—slip next 2 stitches separately and kwise to right needle. Insert left needle into front of these 2 stitches and knit them together
M	with left needle, lift horizontal strand between needles and knit into back of it
/	p2tog—purl next 2 stitches together

Finishing

Cowl and hat: remove needle from last row. Carefully remove waste yarn from beginning edge and position piece with live stitches adjacent to each other. Using the tail, graft ends together using kitchener stitch.

What you have now is a perfectly nice cowl. If a cowl is your final intention, stop now, weave in all loose ends, turn the cowl WS out and lightly steam. For a hat with an asterisk on top, continue.

Bottom Edging

With right sides facing, using smaller circular needle, and beginning at the first stitch of a purl strip, * pick up 9 sts across purl strip, pick up 7 sts across eyelet strip; repeat from * around—80 sts.

Rnd 1: purl around.
Rnd 2: knit around.
Rnds 3 and 4: repeat rnds 1 and 2.

Bind off all sts loosely pwise.

Top Closure

Fold along any A point so that the adjacent B points meet with WS together (Fig. 1, which shows the piece before grafting for clarity).

With RS facing, working through both thicknesses, and using the crochet hook, join yarn with slip stitch in both B points, work 7 single crochets evenly spaced across to point A at fold, single crochet in point A.

Working from left to right, crab stitch in each stitch across back to joined B points.

*Fold hat at next point A, matching up next point B with previously joined B points.

Work 7 single crochets evenly spaced through both thicknesses across to next most recently folded point A, single crochet in point A.

Working from left to right, crab stitch in each stitch back to most recently joined B points; repeat from * around; cut yarn and pull through last loop.

Using tail, weave through B points and pull tightly to close.

Weave in all loose ends, turn WS out and lightly steam.

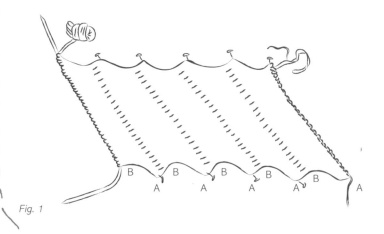

Fig. 1

ELLEN MITERED EARWARMER

Chunky headbands are great, but sometimes you need something a bit more subtle and refined. Ellen is just that. Useful on its own, this earwarmer also works under a bike helmet or hood or even another hat when it's brutally cold out. The button closure ensures a quick on and off.

Skill level ★ ★

Yarn

- Jojoland Rhythm #8-M06 pink, blue, green [100% wool; 110 yds. (100m)/50g]—1 ball

Needles and Notions

- US size 7 (4.5mm) straight needles
- Crochet hook: US-F/5 (3.5mm)
- 1 in. (2.5cm) button (x1)
- Tapestry needle
- Sewing needle and thread

Gauge

- 18 sts and 28 rows = 4 in. (10cm) in St st

Size

- 21½ in. (54.5cm) long x 5¼ in. wide (13.5cm) at widest point

Pattern notes

For this pattern use a different color sewing thread than your yarn color, in case you have to cut the button off. It's easy to see and you won't snip the yarn by mistake.

Cast on 6 sts, leaving a 7 in. (18cm) tail.

Rows 1–4: knit across.

Row 5 (RS): k2, m1right, k2, m1left, k2—8 sts.

Row 6: k3, p2, k3.

Row 7: k3, m1right, k2, m1left, k3—10 sts.

Row 8: k3, p4, k3.

Row 9: k3, m1right, k4, m1left, k3—12 sts.

Row 10: k3, p6, k3.

Row 11: k3, m1right, k6, m1left, k3—14 sts.

Row 12: k3, p8, k3.

Row 13: k3, m1right, k8, m1left, k3—16 sts.

Row 14: k3, p10, k3.

Row 15: k3, m1right, k10, m1left, k3—18 sts.

Row 16: k3, p12, k3.

Row 17: k3, m1right, k12, m1left, k3—20 sts.

Row 18: k3, p14, k3.

Row 19: k3, m1right, k14, m1left, k3—22 sts.

Row 20: k3, p16, k3.

Row 21: k3, m1right, k16, m1left, k3—24 sts.

Row 22: k3, p18, k3.

Row 23: k3, m1right, k18, m1left, k3—26 sts.

Row 24: k3, p20, k3.

Row 25: knit across.

Row 26: k3, p20, k3.

Row 27: k3, m1right, k7, ssk, k2, k2tog, k7, m1left, k3.

Row 28: k3, p20, k3.

Rows 29–66: repeat rows 27 and 28, 19 times.

Row 67: knit across.

Row 68: k3, p20, k3.

Rows 69–72: repeat rows 67 and 68 twice.

Row 73: k2, ssk, k8, m1right, k2, m1left, k8, k2tog, k2.

Row 74: k3, p20, k3.

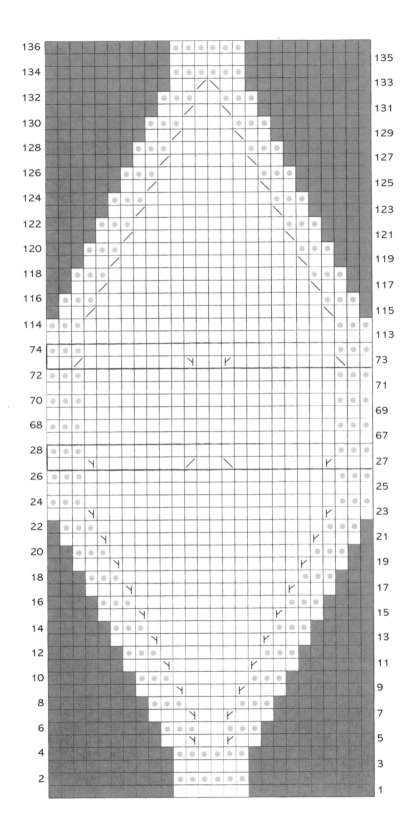

On RS rows, work chart from right to left; On WS rows, work chart from left to right.

▓	no stitch
□	knit on RS rows; purl on WS rows
●	purl on RS rows; knit on WS rows
Y	make 1 right—insert left needle under horizontal strand between stitches from back to front, then knit the front of strand
Y	make 1 left—insert left needle under horizontal strand between stitches from front to back, then knit into back of strand
/	k2tog—knit next 2 stitches together
\	ssk—slip next 2 stitches separately and knitwise to right needle. Insert left needle into the front of these 2 stitches and knit them together
⬚	repeat instructions enclosed in box as many times as specified in written instructions

Rows 75–112: repeat rows 73 and 74, 19 times.

Row 113: knit across.

Row 114: k3, p20, k3.

Row 115: k2, ssk, k18, k2tog, k2—24 sts.

Row 116: k3, p18, k3.

Row 117: k2, ssk, k16, k2tog, k2—22 sts.

Row 118: k3, p16, k3.

Row 119: k2, ssk, k14, k2tog, k2—20 sts.

Row 120: k3, p14, k3.

Row 121: k2, ssk, k12, k2tog, k2—18 sts.

Row 122: k3, p12, k3.

Row 123: k2, ssk, k10, k2tog, k2—16 sts.

Row 124: k3, p10, k3.

Row 125: k2, ssk, k8, k2tog, k2—14 sts.

Row 126: k3, p8, k3.

Row 127: k2, ssk, k6, k2tog, k2—12 sts.

Row 128: k3, p6, k3.

Row 129: k2, ssk, k4, k2tog, k2—10 sts.

Row 130: k3, p4, k3.

Row 131: k2, ssk, k2, k2tog, k2—8 sts.

Row 132: k3, p2, k3.

Row 133: k2, ssk, k2tog, k2—6 sts.

Rows 134–136: knit across.

Bind off all sts until one stitch remains.

Button Loop

Your crochet should be moderately tight. Slip the last stitch onto crochet hook and chain 7 stitches (see Fig. 1).

Fig. 1

Turn the work over so that the WS is facing, insert hook in first bound-off stitch (see Fig. 2), yo hook and draw through the stitch and through the loop on the hook (slip stitch).

Fig. 2

Turn the work over so that the RS is facing and work 12 single crochets into the chain (the button loop, see Fig. 3).

Slip stitch in the same loop, then cut the yarn and fasten off.

Fig. 3

Finishing

Weave in loose ends.

Your earwarmer looks quite peculiar now. It requires washing and blocking to make it flat. Wet the earwarmer completely in a sink using lukewarm water, lather it up gently with bar soap or mild detergent, and squeeze the suds through gently. Rinse twice in the same temperature water, also gently. Place the earwarmer flat on a towel, roll towel up, and squeeze to remove excess water. With the earwarmer on a flat surface, work the piece with your fingers until it is flat, and allow it to dry overnight.

Sew the button on the right side of the beginning end, approximately 4 rows from the end, or more if you want the band to be smaller.

Variation

This pattern also lends itself very nicely to stripes, which highlight the mitered structure in an interesting way.

Simply start with your main color, and then alternate with a contrasting color every two rows, following the pattern as written. Make sure not to pull too tightly at the beginning of the row when you change colors. The edge needs to "breathe."

COZY CABLE HAT

This hat provides the perfect twist to a classic pompom hat. The hat was knit with two shades of red yarn held together to create a more interesting effect. The oversized pompom gives the hat a quirky edge.

Skill level ★ ★

Yarn

- Cygnet superwash DK Raspberry #2151 and Geranium #2185 [100% pure new wool; 113 yds. (104m)/50g]—2 balls of each color

Needles and Notions

- US size 10 16 in. circular needle and set of 5 double pointed needles
- Cable needle
- Tapestry needle

Gauge

- Holding 2 strands of yarn, 14 sts and 18 rows = 4 in. (10cm) in pattern

Size

- 17¼ in. (44cm) circumference x 8¼ in. (21cm) high

Pattern notes

This project is knit with 2 strands of yarn held together to give it a heavier weight. You could substitute a single strand of chunky weight yarn, provided you match the gauge.

Despite the decreasing number of stitches in this pattern, the cables are maintained throughout the shaping of the hat.

Using circular needles and 2 strands of yarn, one of each color, cast on 88 sts; being careful not to twist sts, join to work in rnds. Place marker to mark beginning of rnd.

Rnds 1–6: *p2, k2; repeat from * around.

Rnds 7–12: *p2, k6; repeat from * around.

Rnd 13: *p2, C6B; repeat from * around.

Rnds 14–21: *p2, k6; repeat from * around.

Rnd 22: *p2, C6B; repeat from * around.

Rnds 23–26: *p2, k6; repeat from * around.

Rnd 27: *p2, skp, k2, k2tog; repeat from * around—66 sts.

Rnds 28 and 29: *p2, k4; repeat from * around.

Rnd 30: *p2, C4B; repeat from * around.

Rnds 31–36: *p2, k4; repeat from * around.

Change to double pointed needles.

Rnd 37: *p2, skp, k2tog; repeat from * around—44 sts.

Rnds 38–41: *p2, k2; repeat from * around.

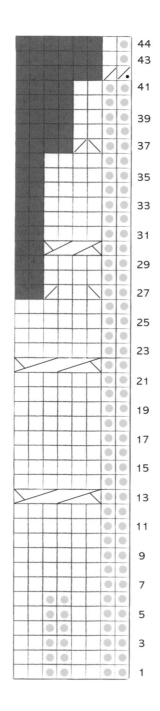

Work chart from right to left, 11 times every round.

☐	knit
■	no stitch
●	purl
╲	skp—slip 1 kwise, k1, pass slipped stitch over
╱	k2tog—knit 2 stitches together
╱•	p2tog—purl next 2 stitches together
﹀﹀	C4B—slip next 2 sts onto cable needle and hold in back of work, k2, k2 from cable needle
﹀﹀	C6B—slip next 3 sts onto cable needle and hold in back of work, k3, k3 from cable needle

Rnd 42: *p2tog, k2tog; repeat from * rep around—22 sts.

Rnds 43 and 44: *p1, k1; repeat from * around.

Finishing

Cut yarn and weave through remaining sts, pulling tightly to close.

How to Make a Pompom

You can use both colors together or just one color if you prefer.

Cut out two circular pieces of cardboard, 3½ in. (9cm) in diameter, with a 1¼ in. (3cm) diameter hole cut in the middle.

With your hands, wrap 2 or more strands of yarn in and out of the center hole, working your way around the pompom ring until the center hole is full.

Carefully cut the yarn around the outside edge of the cardboard, slipping your scissors between the two rings to make the cutting easier.

Pull the rings slightly apart and tie a long length of yarn around the pompom center. Knot tightly.

Pull off the cardboard rings.

Trim yarn ends to shape the pompom. Do not cut the yarn used to tie the pompom—this is used to attach the pompom to the top of the hat.

Sew the pompom securely to the top of the hat.

Weave in loose ends.

TAPROOT SASH

This obi-style belt is extra wide and functions both as a source of warmth and decoration. A narrow knit cord forms the tie, which can be fastened either in front or back depending on your preference. The cable stitch gives the surface the appearance of an elaborate root system growing outward from a central node, hence the name.

Skill level ★ ★

Yarn

- Brown Sheep Lamb's Pride Bulky Charcoal Heather M04 [85% wool, 15% mohair, 125 yds. (114m)/113g]—2 skeins (for all sizes)

Needles and Notions

- US size 11 (8mm) straight needles and set of 2 double pointed needles
- Cable needle
- Tapestry needle

Gauge

- 11 sts and 14 rows = 4 in. (10cm) in St st

Size

- X-Small {Small, Medium, Large}

  7 in. wide x 27 {31, 35, 39} in. long

  18cm wide x 68.5 {79, 89, 99} cm long

Pattern notes

This sash is knit in a graduated cable stitch, beginning at the narrow point and becoming wider. You will be gradually increasing to the full width of the sash by adding stitches at the beginning and end of every RS row. To prevent curling, every row will begin and end with 2 knit stitches, creating a garter stitch border.

Shaping

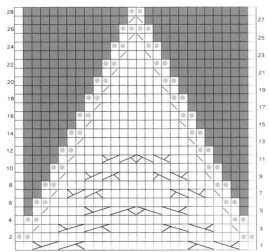

Second Side

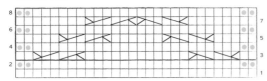

First Side

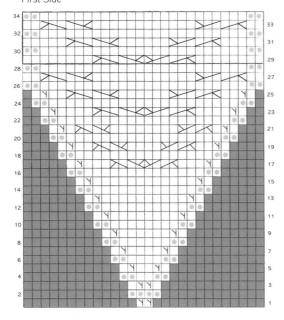

On RS rows, work Chart from right to left; On WS rows work Chart from left to right

☐	knit on RS rows, purl on WS rows
■	no stitch
●	purl on RS rows; knit on WS rows
⅄	kfb—knit into the front and into the back of the next stitch
\	skp—slip 1 kwise, k1, pass slipped stitch over
/	k2tog—knit 2 stitches together
⋎⋏	C4B—slip next 2 sts onto cable needle and hold in back of work, k2, k2 from cable needle
⋋⋎	C4F—slip next 2 sts onto cable needle and hold in front of work, k2, k2 from cable needle
⋎⋏	C6B—slip next 3 sts onto cable needle and hold in back of work, k3, k3 from cable needle
⋋⋎	C6F—slip next 3 sts onto cable needle and hold in front of work, k3, k3 from cable needle
☐	Repeat stitches enclosed in red box as many times as specified in written instructions.

First Cord

Using dpns, cast on 2 sts.

Row 1: k1, k1tbl.

Row 2: slide sts to opposite end of needle, k1, k1tbl.

Repeat row 2 until cord measures 36 in. (91.5cm).

First Side

Change to straight needles.

Row 1 (RS): kfb twice—4 sts.

Row 2: knit across.

Row 3: k1, kfb twice, k1—6 sts.

Row 4: k2, purl across to last 2 sts, k2.

Row 5: k1, kfb, knit across to last 2 sts, kfb, k1—8 sts.

Rows 6-16: repeat rows 4 and 5, 5 times, then repeat row 4 once more—18 sts.

Row 17: k1, kfb, k3, C4B, C4F, k3, kfb, k1—20 sts.

Row 18 and all WS rows through row 34: k2, purl across to last 2 sts, k2.

Row 19: k1, kfb, k2, C4B, k4, C4F, k2, kfb, k1—22 sts.

Row 21: k1, kfb, k1, C4B, k8, C4F, k1, kfb, k1—24 sts.

Row 23: k1, kfb, k4, C6B, C6F, k4, kfb, k1—26 sts.

Row 25: k1, kfb, k2, C6B, k6, C6F, k2, kfb, k1—28 sts.

Row 27: k2, C6B, k12, C6F, k2.

Row 29: k8, C6B, C6F, k8.

Row 31: k5, C6B, k6, C6F, k5.

Row 33: k2, C6B, k12, C6F, k2.

Repeat rows 29–34, 1 {2, 3, 4} times.

Second Side

Row 1: knit across.

Row 2 and all WS rows through row 8: k2, purl across to last 2 sts, k2.

Row 3: K2, C6F, k12, C6B, k2.

Row 5: K5, C6F, k6, C6B, k5.

Row 7: K8, C6F, C6B, k8.

Repeat rows 3–8, 1 {2, 3, 4} times.

Shaping

Row 1: K2, C6F, k12, C6B, k2.

Row 2 and all WS rows through row 24: k2, purl across to last 2 sts, k2.

Row 3: K1, skp, k2, C6F, k6, C6B, k2, k2tog, k1—26 sts.

Row 5: K1, skp, k4, C6F, C6B, k4, k2tog, k1—24 sts.

Row 7: K1, skp, k1, C4F, k8, C4B, k1, k2tog, k1—22 sts.

Row 9: K1, skp, k2, C4F, k4, C4B, k2, k2tog, k1—20 sts.

Row 11: K1, skp, k3, C4F, C4B, k3, k2tog, k1—18 sts.

Row 13 and all RS rows through row 23: k1, skp, knit across to last 3 sts, k2tog, k1—6 sts.

Row 25: k1, skp, k2tog, k1—4 sts.

Row 26: knit across.

Row 27: skp, k2tog—2 sts.

Row 28: knit across.

Second Cord

Slip the 2 remaining sts onto a dpn and repeat row 2 of the First Cord until Second Cord measures 36 in. (91.5cm).

Bind off all sts knitwise.

Weave in loose ends.

Finishing

Blocking is really important for this piece. Let the sash sit in a sink full of hot water until it sinks to the bottom. Squeeze water out by hand or by rolling up in a towel to remove as much moisture as possible. Lay the sash flat, sculpting into shape and flattening out the edges, pinning as needed.

NORDIC SNOWFLAKE EARFLAP HAT

This Nordic-style hat may take patience to knit because it combines knitting in the round with a Fair Isle pattern, but it is well worth the effort. The earflaps will keep you warm and the ties keep the hat from blowing away. This is a funky little hat for any snow lover. You can pair it with the Nordic Snowflake Mittens (see page 134).

Skill level ★ ★

Yarn

- Cygnet Superwash DK, Cream #2195 (MC); Bluebell #2156 (Color A); Everglade #2817 (Color B) [100% pure new wool; 113 yds. (104m)/50g]—1 skein of Cream and Bluebell, 5 yds. (4.5m) of Everglade

Needles and Notions

- US size 10 (6mm) straight needles, 16 in. circular needle and set of 5 double pointed needles
- Stitch holder (x2)
- Stitch marker
- Tapestry needle

Gauge

- Holding 2 strands of yarn, 14 sts and 20 rows = 4 in. (10cm) in St st

Size

- 19½ in. (49.5cm) circumference x 10½ in. (26.5cm) high unstretched

Pattern notes

Make sure that the tension of your knitting remains consistent. It is easy to knit too tightly when working the color pattern, causing the hat to pull in, and resulting in a hat that won't stretch over your head.

This hat is knit with 2 strands of yarn to make the fabric thicker.

Snowflake pattern The snowflake pattern is worked over 17 stitches and 19 rounds.

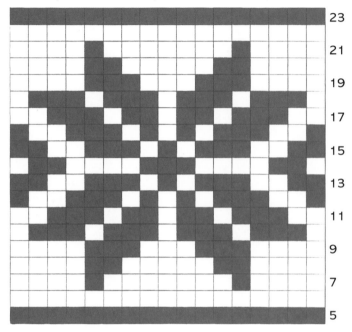

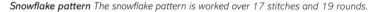

For Hat, work Chart from right to left 4 times on every round. For Mittens (page 134), work Chart 2 times in every row, working from right to left on RS rows and left to right on WS rows.

Rnds 1–4: knit around.

Rnds 5–23: change to 2 strands of Color A (do NOT cut MC) and begin working Chart. Follow chart for 19 rnds; cut Color A.

Rnds 24–26: change to 2 strands of MC and knit 3 rnds.

Crown

Change to double pointed needles when circular needle becomes too long for the number of stitches.

Rnd 1: k2, *k2tog, k9; repeat from * around—62 sts.

Rnd 2: knit around.

Rnd 3: k2, *k2tog, k8; repeat from * around—56 sts.

Rnd 4: knit around.

Continue decreasing 6 sts in same manner, every other round, until 14 sts remain.

Earflaps (Make 2)

Using straight needles and 2 strands of MC, cast on 9 sts.

Row 1 (WS): k1, p to last st, k1.

Row 2: k1, kfb, k to last 2 sts, kfb, k1—11 sts.

Rows 3–6: repeat rows 1 and 2 twice—15 sts.

Row 7: k1, p to last st, k1.

Row 8: knit across.

Rows 9–15: repeat rows 7 and 8, 3 times, then repeat row 7 once more.

Cut yarn; slip sts onto st holder and set aside.

Repeat for second earflap.

Body

Using circular needles and two strands of MC, cast on 8 sts; k15 from first ear flap, cast on 22 sts, k15 from second ear flap, cast on 8 sts; being careful not to twist sts, join to work in the rnd. Place marker to mark the beginning of the rnd—68 sts.

Finishing

Cut yarn and weave through remaining sts, pulling tightly to close. Weave in loose ends.

Measure approximately 1 yd. (1m) of each color.

Thread each strand through the mid point of bottom edge of earflap.

Braid the 6 strands to desired length.

Knot end and trim.

Repeat for second braid on other earflap.

With Color B, work blanket st around the lower edge of hat and earflaps.

Turn WS out and steam lightly.

Get it Right!

You may notice that in the corner of each earflap, there are small holes. Don't worry about this, as they will be covered up when you add blanket stitches around the edge.

NORDIC SNOWFLAKE MITTENS

These Nordic mittens are knit with two strands of yarn, so they will keep your hands super-cozy and warm. Wearing mittens brings out the child in all of us, and these are designed in the Scandinavian style to be worn large—to make you feel extra-childlike. Like the Nordic Snowflake Earflap Hat (see page 130), these may take a bit of time to make, but your hands will thank you!

Skill level ★ ★ ★

Yarn

- Cygnet Superwash DK, Cream #2195 (MC); Bluebell #2156 (Color A); Everglade #2817 (Color B) [100% pure new wool; 113 yds. (104m)/50g]—1 skein of Cream and Bluebell, 5 yds. (4.5m) of Everglade

Needles and Notions

- US size 10 (6mm) straight needles, set of 2 double pointed needles (check size information first to ensure you select right size for your hands)
- Tapestry needle

Gauge

- Holding 2 strands of yarn, 16 sts and 20 rows = 4 in. (10cm) in St st

Size

- 8 in. (20cm) palm circumference x 12 in. (30cm) long
- One size fits most as these are meant to be large. For smaller sizes, change your gauge and needles as follows:
- For palm circumference of 7 in. (18cm), use US size 8 (5mm) needles and a gauge of 18 sts and 24 rows = 4 in. (10cm)
- For palm circumference of 7½ in. (19cm), use US size 9 (5.5mm) needles and a gauge of 17 sts and 22 rows = 4 in. (10cm)

Left Mitten

Using straight needles and 2 strands throughout for both colors, cast on 34 sts with MC.

Row 1 (WS): purl across.

Rows 2–20: working in St st, change to Color A and follow Chart (see page 132), rows 5–23.

Thumb Gusset

Row 21: with MC, k12, p1, kfb, kfb, k1, p1, k17—36 sts.

Row 22: p17, k1, p5, k1, p12.

Row 23: k12, p1, k5, p1, k17.

Row 24: p17, k1, p5, k1, p12.

Row 25: k12, p1, kfb, k2, kfb, k1, p1, k17—38 sts.

Row 26: p17, k1, p7, k1, p12.

Row 27: k12, p1, k7, p1, k17.

Row 28: p17, k1, p7, k1, p12.

Row 29: k12, p1, kfb, k4, kfb, k1, p1, k17—40 sts.

Row 30: p17, k1, p9, k1, p12.

Row 31: k12, p1, k9, p1, k17.

Row 32: p17, k1, p9, k1, p12.

Row 33: k12, p1, kfb, k6, kfb, k1, p1, k17—42 sts.

Row 34: p17, k1, p11, k1, p12.

Thumb

Row 1: k25; turn, leaving remaining sts unworked.

Row 2: cast on 1 st, purl cast on st and next 13 sts; turn—14 sts.

Row 3: cast on 1 st, knit cast on st and next 14 sts; turn—15 sts.

Rows 4–12: work in St st for 9 rows.

Row 13: k1, (k2 tog) across—8 sts.

Cut yarn and weave through remaining sts, pulling tightly to close.

With same tail, sew thumb seam.

Mitten Hand

With MC and using remaining unworked sts, continue as follows:

Row 35: pick up 5 sts at the base of the thumb, knit to end of row—34 sts.

Row 36: purl across.

Rows 37–48: work in St st for 12 rows or until 2 {2¼ , 2½} in. (5 {5.75, 6.25} cm) less than desired length.

Top Shaping

With MC, continue as follows:

Row 49: k1, skp, k11, k2tog, k2, skp, k11, k2tog, k1—30 sts.

Row 50: purl across.

Row 51: k1, skp, k9, k2tog, k2, skp, K9, k2tog, k1—26 sts.

Row 52: purl across.

Row 53: k1, skp, k7, k2tog, k2, skp, K7, k2tog, k1—22 sts.

Row 54: purl across.

Row 55: k1, skp, k5, k2tog, k2, skp, K5, k2tog, k1—18 sts.

Row 56: purl across.

Row 57: k1, skp, k3, k2tog, k2, skp, K3, k2tog, k1—14 sts.

Row 58: purl across.

Row 59: k1, skp, k1, k2tog, k2, skp, k1, k2tog, k1—10 sts.

Slip first 5 sts onto double pointed needle, slip next 5 sts onto second double pointed needle. Fold mitten in half with wrong sides together. Insert straight needle through first st on front needle and through first st on back needle and k2tog. Repeat in next st on front and back needles, pass second st on right needle over first st on same needle. Work across remaining sts in same manner.

Cut yarn leaving 18 in. (46cm) tail for sewing and pull through last st.

With same tail, weave side seam using mattress stitch.

Right Mitten

Using straight needles and 2 strands throughout for both colors, cast on 34 sts with MC.

Row 1: purl across.

Rows 2–20: working in St st, change to Color A and follow Chart (see page 132), rows 5–23.

Thumb Gusset

Row 21: with MC, k17, p1, kfb, kfb, k1, p1, k12—36 sts.

Row 22: p12, k1, p5, k1, p17.

Row 23: k17, p1, k5, p1, k12.

Row 24: p12, k1, p5, k1, p17.

Row 25: k17, p1, kfb, k2, kfb, k1, p1, k12—38 sts.

Row 26: p12, k1, p7, k1, p17.

Row 27: k17, p1, k7, p1, k12.

Row 28: p12, k1, p7, k1, p17.

Row 29: k17, p1, kfb, k4, kfb, k1, p1, k12—40 sts.

Row 30: p12, k1, p9, k1, p17.

Row 31: k17, p1, k9, p1, k12.

Row 32: p12, k1, p9, k1, p17.

Row 33: k17, p1, kfb, k6, kfb, k1, p1, k12—42 sts.

Row 34: p12, k1, p11, k1, p17.

Thumb

Row 1: k30; turn, leaving remaining sts unworked.

Complete same as Left Mitten, beginning with row 2 of Thumb.

Finishing—Both Mittens

With Color B, work blanket stitch around the wrist of each mitten.

Weave in loose ends.

Turn WS out and steam lightly.

HA'PENNY LOOP COWL

The Ha'Penny Loop is a warm, useful, and very dramatic cowl. It can be used as a long scarf, or twisted over the head for use as a hood and scarf combo in inclement weather. The simple six-stitch repeat gives a 3D effect of one net laid over another, held together by the twisted rib edges.

Skill level ★ ★

Yarn

- Lana Grossa Chiara, #07 rust [70% Viscose Rayon, 20% Superkid Mohair, 10% Polyamid; 209 yds. (190m)/50g]—8 balls

Needles and Notions

- US size 11 24 in. circular needle
- Tapestry needle
- Stitch marker

Gauge

- Holding 4 strands of yarn, 12 sts and 16 rows = 4 in. (10cm) in St st.

Gauge is not critical on this piece, as long as the result is a drapey and soft fabric.

Size

- 60 in. (152.5cm) circumference x 11 in. (28cm) wide

Pattern notes

This project is a gentle introduction into circular lace, but you need to pay close attention to the starting stitch on each row of the lace (see Chart, page 140, for details.)

The Ha'Penny Loop is knit using 4 strands of "Chiara" held together. If you substitute yarn, the resulting fabric should be soft, not stiff.

For an extra-wide, luxurious loop, buy an extra 4 balls, and knit another repeat of the lace section (for a total of 3 lace repeats), rows 10–25, before knitting the ending rib.

Holding 4 strands of yarn together, loosely cast on 180 sts. Place marker to mark beginning of rnd.

Beginning Ribbing

Rnd 1 (RS): k1, p1, *k2, p1; repeat from * around to last st, k1.

Rnd 2: slip 1 pwise wyib, p1, *C2F, p1; repeat from * around to last st, C2F using first st of rnd, keeping marker between 2 sts.

Rnd 3: p1, *k2, p1; repeat from * around to last st, k1.

Rnds 4–9: repeat rnds 2 and 3, 3 times.

Lace

Rnd 10: *ssk, k1, yo twice, k1, k2tog; repeat from * around.

Rnd 11: k3, p1, *k5, p1; repeat from * around to last 2 sts, k2.

Rnd 12: *yo twice, ssk, k2, k2tog; repeat from * around.

Rnd 13: k1, p1, *k5, p1; repeat from * around to last 4 sts, k4.

Rnd 14: *k2, yo, ssk, k2tog, yo; repeat from * around.

Rnd 15: knit around.

Rnd 16: slip 1 pwise wyib, *k2tog, yo, k2, yo, ssk; repeat from * around, working last ssk with first st of round 17.

Rnd 17: knit around.

Rnd 18: *yo twice, k1, k2tog, ssk, k1; repeat from * around.

Rnd 19: k1, p1, *k5, p1; repeat from * around to last 4 sts, k4.

Rnd 20: *k2, k2tog, yo twice, ssk; repeat from * around.

Rnd 21: k4, p1, *k5, p1; repeat from * around to last st, k1.

Rnd 22: *k2tog, yo, k2, yo, ssk; repeat from * around.

Rnd 23: knit around.

Rnd 24: k1, yo, ssk, k2tog, yo, *k2, yo, ssk, k2tog, yo; repeat from * around to last st, k1.

Rnd 25: knit around.

Rnds 26–41: repeat rnds 10–25.

Ending Ribbing

Rnd 42: *p1, C2F; repeat from * around.

Rnd 43: *p1, k2; repeat from * around.

Rnds 44–48: repeat rnds 42 and 43 twice, then repeat rnd 42 once more.

Bind off all sts loosely in pattern.

Finishing

Weave in loose ends.

Turn WS out and steam lightly.

INDEX

Credits

Laura Long (Isabela Bolero, Ribbed Flowers, Midnight Cable Scarf, Posy Striped Slippers, Chloe Purl or Knit Vest, Daisy Lined Purse, Daisy Reversible Bag, Chunky Check Collar, Cozy Cable Hat, Nordic Snowflake Earflap Hat, Nordic Snowflake Mittens)
Melissa Halvorson (Hook-and-Eye Clover Legwarmers, Smoke and Mirrors Smock, Taproot Sash)
Kim Hamlin (Retro Angle Scarf)
Staceyjoy Elkin (Belladonna Opera-Length Fingerless Mitts, Nine of Diamonds Capelet, Lauren Woven Belt, Jutta Beret, Chrysalis Shrug, Sydney Cabled Legwarmers, A Flock of Seagulls Wristlets, Tepee Slouch Hat, Ellen Mitered Earwarmer, Ha'Penny Loop Cowl)

Designer: Jon Wainwright and Sharanjit Dhol
Illustrator: Stefanie Coltra
Photographer: Sussie Ahlburg
Retro Angle Scarf photography: Kim Hamlin
Taproot Sash photography: Melissa Halvorson

Models: Genevieve Carden, Nicola Coates, Stefanie Coltra, Margarita Lievano Mosquera, Mafalda Satz, Marisa Wasboonma

Yarn Manufacturers

The following list gives web addresses for all of the yarn manufacturers whose yarns appear in this book:

alchemyyarns.com
blueskyalpacas.com
brownsheep.com
cascadeyarns.com
cygnetyarns.com
jojoland.com
karabellayarns.com
knitpicks.com
lanagrossa.com
lanaknits.com
lavishfibres.com
malabrigoyarn.com
manos.com.uy
mistialpaca.com
www.sirdar.co.uk